William Carlos Williams's Early Poetry

The Visual Arts Background

Studies in Modern Literature, No. 35

A. Walton Litz, General Series Editor

Professor of English
Princeton University

Paul Mariani

Consulting Editor for Titles on William Carlos Williams
Professor of English
University of Massachusetts/Amherst

Other Titles in This Series

William Carlos Williams's Early Poetry
The Visual Arts Background

by
Christopher J. MacGowan

UMI RESEARCH PRESS
Ann Arbor, Michigan

Copyright © 1984, 1983
Christopher John MacGowan
All rights reserved

Produced and distributed by
UMI Research Press
an imprint of
University Microfilms International
Ann Arbor, Michigan 48106

Library of Congress Cataloging in Publication Data

MacGowan, Christopher J. (Christopher John)
William Carlos Williams's early poetry.

(Studies in modern literature ; no. 35)
"A revision of the author's thesis, Princeton,
University, 1983"–T.p. verso.
Bibliography: p.
Includes index.
1. Williams, William Carlos, 1883-1963–Knowledge–
Art. 2. Art and literature. 3. Painting in literature.
I. Title. II. Series.

PS3545.I544Z626 1984   811'.52   83-24280
ISBN 0-8357-1522-1

2317429

For my father

Contents

List of Illustrations

List of Abbreviations

The following abbreviations are used in the text:

ARI   *A Recognizable Image: William Carlos Williams on Art and Artists,* ed. with an introduction by Bram Dijkstra (New York: New Directions, 1978).

Auto   *The Autobiography of William Carlos Williams* (New York: Random House, 1951).

CEP   *The Collected Earlier Poems of William Carlos Williams* (New York: New Directions, 1951).

CLP   *The Collected Later Poems of William Carlos Williams* (New York: New Directions, 1963).

IAG   *In the American Grain* (1925; rpt. New York: New Directions, 1966).

IWWP   *I Wanted to Write a Poem: The Autobiography of the Works of a Poet,* reported and ed. by Edith Heal (1958; rev. ed. New York: New Directions, 1967).

EK   *The Embodiment of Knowledge,* ed. with an introduction by Ron Loewinsohn (New York: New Directions, 1974).

Imag   *Imaginations,* ed. with introductions by Webster Schott (New York: New Directions, 1970).

Pat   *Paterson* (New York: New Directions, 1963).

PB   *Pictures from Brueghel* (New York: New Directions, 1962).

SE   *Selected Essays of William Carlos Williams* (New York: Random House, 1954).

SL   *The Selected Letters of William Carlos Williams,* ed. John C. Thirlwall (New York: McDowell, Obolensky, 1957).

Acknowledgments

During the research and writing of this study I have been helped by many people. I thank A. Walton Litz for introducing me to the work of Williams, and for his unstinting support and advice at every stage of this study. I also thank Ted Weiss and Paul Mariani for their encouragement and helpful comments on my manuscript. Emily Wallace was kind enough to discuss Williams's interest in painting with me, and William Marling, Judith Zilczer, and Harold Diamond clarified a number of issues through correspondence.

I am grateful to James Laughlin and Peggy L. Fox of the New Directions Publishing Corporation, and also to the staffs of the following institutions for their help and cooperation: the Beinecke Library, Yale University; the British Library; the Rare Book and Manuscript Library, Columbia University; Fairleigh Dickinson University Library; the Lilly Library, Indiana University; the Lockwood Memorial Library, SUNY Buffalo; the New York Public Library; Princeton University Library; the Manuscript Department, University of Virginia Library.

Finally, I am indebted to Elizabeth Witherell for her kindness and support.

Preface

When Ezra Pound wrote to William Carlos Williams in 1908 defending his *A Lume Spento* from his friend's charge of "poetic anarchy," he called Williams's attention to "what the poets and musicians *and* painters are doing with a good deal of convention that has masqueraded as law" (Pound's emphasis). Pound's letter gives evidence of what he was gaining from an interest in the painters: he scoffs at the demands of "the public," dismisses the traditional subject matter of verse, and declares "sometimes I use rules of Spanish, Anglo-Saxon and Greek metric that are not common in the English of Milton's or Miss Austen's day."[1] The modernist painters had already, by this date, developed similar strategies for painting. In fact, the "law" that painters such as Cézanne, Whistler and Kandinsky had challenged covered almost every aspect of their art.

The painters asserted that painting was first and foremost a matter of paint upon canvas—not 'a mirror up to nature' or 'a window on the world.' The painter, no longer feeling bound to the conventions that dictated form and subject matter, could explore new themes and patterns. These themes and patterns were centered on the essential properties of his medium—color and spatial relationships. The painter no longer needed to heed the claims of his audience. Control of the artifact returned to the artist, and in his insistence upon its status as artifact he could demand from his audience, instead of having to meet its demands.

The modernist poets were also drawn to the strategies of the painters by the nature of the modernist poetic. Poetry was no longer to concern itself with action and narrative; now it expressed—in the words of T. E. Hulme—"expression and communication of momentary phases in the poet's mind." Expression was to be structured through juxtaposition, "two visual images form what one may call a visual chord. They unite to suggest an image which is different to both."[2] The build-up of pattern in a Cézanne or Kandinsky painting was similarly through the accumulation of "visual chords."

The years 1909 through 1925 were marked in New York, Paris and

London by an unparalleled collaboration between the poets and the painters. The "little magazines" published reproductions of modernist and
"primitive" art alongside prose and poetry. Poets painted and painters
wrote. Poets cited painters in their manifestoes, and painters wrote out
their painterly theories and incorporated linguistic elements into the visual strategies of their paintings. This study is an exploration of William
Carlos Williams's part in the collaboration. Perhaps more than any other
poet, Williams looked to painting for new strategies to bring to his work.
The development of his early poetry is the development of an increasingly
complex series of patterns—within poems, and within sequences of
poems—leading up to his 1923 *Spring and All,* dedicated to the painter
Charles Demuth.

In writing this study I have had two main concerns. The first is to
document, where possible, Williams's contact with painters and theories
within the modernist visual arts; the second is to apply this background
material to a careful study of the poems themselves. The first two chapters
deal largely with Williams's response to Pound's work and to the magazines associated with Pound. They cover the 1909 *Poems, The Tempers,*
and a number of the *Al Que Quiere!* poems. Chapter Three also discusses
Al Que Quiere!, and explores Williams's growing involvement with the
New York avant-garde. Chapter Four examines *Kora in Hell: Improvisations* and its important "Prologue," together with its background of
Marcel Duchamp's "ready-mades" and Kandinsky's *Improvisations.* With
his next volume, *Sour Grapes,* Williams turned to a demand for "local"
expression, and this interest, together with his collaboration with Marsden
Hartley and Robert McAlmon on the magazine *Contact,* forms the subject
of Chapter Five. Chapter Six discusses *Spring and All* in terms of its chief
sources—Dada, the American "local" movement, Juan Gris, and the
precisionists—then closely examines a number of individual poems, and
diagrams several of the multiple patterns behind the book's twenty-seven
poems and interspersed prose.

1

1909 *Poems* and *The Tempers*

Discussions of William Carlos Williams's interest in the visual arts tend to begin with the impact of the 1913 New York Armory Show upon the poet. But the famous exhibition is not the landmark in his career that Williams later claimed. He did not attend the show; his interest in painters and his adaptation of painterly ideas to his poetic strategy are evident in his writings before 1913; and Ezra Pound's letters of news in London remained an important influence upon his work beyond that date. A more accurate and useful sense of the visual arts background to Williams's early poetry is gained by setting aside the red herring of the Armory Show, and starting with his earliest poetry and his important early relationships with his brother Edgar, Charles Demuth, and Pound.

Williams encountered both Demuth and Pound while a student at the University of Pennsylvania, and thus began two life-long friendships. The meeting with Demuth occurred over a dish of prunes at Mrs. Chain's boarding house on Locust Street—an incident Williams was fond of recalling. At the time Demuth was enrolled at the city's Drexel Institute, transferring in 1905 to the Pennsylvania Academy of Fine Arts. Another painter whose work would be of great importance to Williams—Charles Sheeler—studied at the Academy at the same time, but he and Demuth saw little of each other, and Williams did not meet Sheeler until the early twenties.

Demuth enthusiastically endorsed Williams's college writing efforts. In a 1907 letter he declared, "I have always felt that it would happen to you some day—that you would simply have to write."[1] Williams reciprocated with an interest in his friend's painting. In a 1956 interview he told Emily Farnham, Demuth's biographer, "Charlie gave me one of his first paintings. It was mostly yellow and lavender, a picture of a girl, and it wasn't any good. I gave it later on to Mrs. Demuth."[2] In addition to this yellow and lavender girl, Williams owned two further examples of his friend's early work. Demuth presented the watercolor *April Landscape*

(c. 1911) as a wedding gift to the Williamses in 1912. Farnham describes this work as "trees treated in Impressionist manner." The other painting, *The Gossips* (c. 1914), she lists as "four figures seated on beach, all but one presenting back to observer. Darkest darks in hats and blouses located in upper half."[3]

A number of Demuth's earliest paintings fit Williams's description of the yellow and lavender girl; most of his canvases until about 1913 continued to be realistic treatments of figure and landscape themes. Although the painter visited Europe for five months in 1907, it was not until his second trip, from December 1912 to the spring of 1914, that he encountered modernist artists and began to develop his characteristic mature style. It was on this visit (through which he missed the Armory Show) that he met Ezra Pound and another figure crucial to Williams—Marsden Hartley. Demuth spent some time in Berlin with Hartley and the sculptor Arnold Rönnebeck. This visit, rather than the time spent in Paris, appears initially to have had the greatest impact upon him. His first one-man show, at the Daniel Gallery in 1914, was almost certainly of "nonobjective paintings produced under the influence of Kandinsky."[4] As this study will demonstrate, in these years Kandinsky's writing and painting has an important place in the thinking not only of Demuth, but also of Williams, Hartley and Pound.[5]

Williams shared both literary and painterly interests with his friend, for in these early years Demuth was thinking seriously of a writing career. His unpublished manuscripts include a number of poems, stories and plays—the little magazine *The Glebe* published his play *The Azure Ladder* in 1913. Williams's letters from this period are full of enthusiastic references to his own dramatic works-in-progress.

Williams remembered of Demuth's writing that "he had a style reminiscent of Whistler's, whom I have reason to believe he sedulously copied" (*Auto,* 151). And he mentioned Whistler again when asked by Emily Farnham: "What artists did Demuth speak favorably of in your presence?" Whereas her other interviewees, such as Marcel Duchamp, Stuart Davis, and the gallery owner Charles Daniel, mentioned the Stieglitz group or the Paris modernists, Williams replied "Whistler and the Japanese."[6] The answer may seem surprising in the light of Demuth's subsequent modernist career, but it is significant in the context of painter and poet fusing their early interests. "From Whistler and the Japanese," Pound wrote in 1914, "the 'world,' that is to say, the fragment of the English-speaking world that spreads itself into print, learned to enjoy 'arrangements' of colors and masses."[7] Over the following twenty years Williams would come to own a number of Demuth's works, and shared ideas and friendships would be important to both men. In 1923, when

Williams published the most successful "arrangement" to come out of his interest in painting—the poems and prose of *Spring and All*—he dedicated the book to his first artistic confidant, Demuth.

Williams had been exposed to painterly interests even before his friendship with Demuth, for his mother painted, and had studied art in Paris. "Her interest in art became my interest in art" (*IWWP,* 16) he later claimed, and this interest is expressed in his earliest letters. Writing from the University of Pennsylvania in 1904, he told his mother of a visit to a local painter, a Mr. Wilson, who "was painting in his studio so he gave me an easel, some brushes and I painted a still life."[8] In his autobiography Williams identified this early teacher as "John Wilson . . . a man in his early fifties, I imagine . . . a failure of an artist who used to paint, right out of his head, landscapes and cows, pictures 24 × 36 inches or so, that sold as 'art' for from ten to twenty dollars" (*Auto,* 61). At the time of the publication of his first book of poems in 1909, he would journey "into the fields along the river . . . to do some painting as Mr. Wilson had taught me" (*Auto,* 106).

Little work survives as evidence of this early activity. In the 1950s, when Yale librarian Norman Holmes Pearson questioned Williams on his early painting efforts and suggested including a canvas or two in the Yale collection, Williams depreciated their importance. Although he "painted a little at one time," he told Pearson, "the results are not enlightening, not worth owning." He offered Pearson the landscape oil *The Passaic River* (warning that the painting was "no good") and also what he called "a bold self-portrait" that has some "light in it."[9] (The landscape c. 1912 is now at Yale; the portrait c. 1914 is at the University of Pennsylvania.) Apart from these two canvases, there remain a few scattered line drawings among Williams's papers at Yale and Buffalo, and some drawings in his 1906 medical class yearbook. This yearbook, on which Williams served as "art editor," contains four line drawings signed "W. C. Williams."

Mrs. Williams's interest in art was also transmitted to Williams's younger brother Edgar, who was painting and drawing in college. In early letters to Edgar, William often asks for news of his work. In 1904, he writes, "Tell me what you do in the art line every time you write to me for I am very much interested". Four years later he is still adding "Tell me about your drawings".[10] Williams's son, William Eric, has described the many paintings on the walls of the Williamses' house at 9 Ridge Road, Rutherford, New Jersey, and noted that among the Hartleys, Demuths, and Sheelers "the majority . . . are water colors done by Dad's brother Edgar."[11]

By 1908 Williams was working as an intern in New York. He told Edgar of his rigorous scheme of self-education, which included studying the plants and trees in Bronx Park, visiting the Museum of Natural History, and attending a lecture course on great masters of music. He also explored the Metropolitan Museum, reporting that "with a catalogue I'll soon be able to distinguish a few of the leading characteristics of the principal schools of painting." This eclectic activity was part of his determination, he told Edgar, to "show the world something more beautiful than it has ever seen before." It was all carefully copied down; "I am keeping notes on architecture, landscape and decoration as well as mechanical features which I like in connection with my idea".[12]

By the following year the synthesis had a more avowedly moral purpose. Williams quoted Milton to Edgar approvingly: "to feel is living and all poetry must be sensuous." Through its affective powers—powers shared by architecture and the other arts—poetry achieves its moral ends: "This is the province of art, to influence the best and as we learn the better and better to influence each other with beauty so shall we perhaps grow to help others and perhaps who can tell in the end we may help many."[13]

Early in 1909 Williams published his first volume of poetry, *Poems,* a small pamphlet of twenty-seven conventional verses that he later disowned and refused to include in his *Collected Poems.* That summer he journeyed to Leipzig to pursue his medical studies. Viewing "the German art" in terms of his apotheosis of feeling, he found it to be "quite ponderous," for all its foundation in "German thought and independence." This "thought" he criticized as lacking any "spontaneity or something akin to innocence and joyousness" (*SL,* 18).

"Innocence" is an important value for Williams in his *Poems.* He conceives of it as having an immutable, transcendent existence. The first line of the first poem declares

> Innocence can never perish. . . .

In another poem from the volume—"The Uses of Poetry"—he views verse as the vehicle to reach a world where such immutability is possible. It is merely the limitations of "sense" which produce the essentially transient feelings of discord and pain.

> We'll draw the light latch-string
> And close the door of sense; then satiate wend,
> On poesy's transforming giant wing,
> To worlds afar whose fruits all anguish mend.

"A Street Market, N.Y., 1908" begins with the announcement of a breakthrough in perception.

> Eyes that can see,
> Oh what a rarity!
> For many a year gone by
> I've looked and nothing seen
> But ever been
> Blind to a patent wide reality.

But this "reality" is one of Platonic universals, and removes the colorful bustle of the market from any specific place and time. We are again in the tranquil world beyond change. The new vision incorporates all races and climes; "thick souls ebb and flow" in a world removed from the limitations of temporal classification. Instead of the intercourse of the particular market, the poet can now see that "History / Welds her gold threads in glittering / brilliant show."

The idealistic impulse behind the poem does not allow the visual emphasis to rest upon the particular. Quite the reverse, conventional diction and personification—felt as necessary to express the all-encompassing "idea"—replace specific description. The argument in "The Bewilderment of Youth" is similar. The bewilderment of the title comes from the bombardment of "myriad . . . forms" upon the sight. With old age and experience this "formless rout" is reduced to "but aspects . . . of scant things true." Finally a Platonic harmony is realized as

> he sees, when life is almost done,
> These final few go mingling into one.

These poems constantly insist upon a dichotomy between the ephemeral particulars and the timeless universal, but in Williams's later work this dichotomy is resolved. The all-encompassing "moment" of *Spring and All,* for example, is preserved in the complex patterning of the work's own unique relationships. Unity is achieved through an unflinching focus upon the particular, allowing the particular to remain sharply delineated while simultaneously assuming its place within the composition's wider patterns.

But this lesson, learned from the painters Hartley, Demuth, Sheeler and Juan Gris, was yet to come. The "reality" that frequently climaxes the poems of the 1909 volume is a visionary haven beyond the ephemeral, particular manifestations of everyday life. It was as the painter of such a "silent" and "fairy-like" world that Williams saw the English painter Turner in a 1909 letter to Edgar. The weather in the English Channel on the voyage to Europe, he told his brother, exhibited the "most wonderful J. M. W. Turner skies—you know the kind with little frost-like fingers pointing at all angles for a background." There is no torrent of detail to cause the spectator "bewilderment," for the central object is isolated by a surrounding mist: "around the horizon was a transparent sunny-looking mist through which the shore shone almost fairy-like, it was so silent, so dim and yet so green and white and beautiful" (*SL,* 15).[14] Williams's association of "green" with this ideal world mirrors the dominant color of many Pre-Raphaelite paintings. Pound uses the same color to characterize an early Williams's poem—"W. C. W.'s Romance"— in his 1908 San Travaso Notebook.

> Oh hale green song,
> . . . after-dream thing of
> old minstrelsy.[15]

And in a letter to Williams he suggested, "perhaps you like pictures painted in green and white and gold and I paint in black and crimson and purple?"[16]

Turner painted many canvases that were far from tranquil, and Williams was fast discovering this and other alternatives to his "green song". Leaving Leipzig in March 1910, he visited Pound in London for a week. Pound wrote home, "I took him to see Yeats on Monday and crammed him with Turner and other such during the rest of the time."[17] After this it was on to Italy and the guidance of Edgar, whom Williams credits with "introducing me to the wonders of medieval and renaissance architecture and painting" (*Auto,* 120). Finally, after Spain—"Madrid and the Goyas" (*Auto,* 124)—Williams returned home to Rutherford.

Williams's 1910 poem "Min Schleppner" retains the dichotomy between the world of appearances and the "reality" beyond them. But instead of this vision of "reality" coming with old age, or through an easy reverie, here the climatic "Sees!" is won out of a hard struggle. The rhythms of the poem parallel this new tension. Instead of merely positing the immutable "reality" and contrasting it with the world of immediate appearance, Williams dramatizes a mode of perception and contrasts it with the distractions that it sees beyond. The way of seeing becomes the controlling force, "fixed," shaping the poem out of chaos.

> Gaunt, my hope, horse-wise
> He sees with wide, half-glazed eyes
> That neither blink, turn aside nor blaze,
> Fixed as we plough the cold haze.
> Round me the ruinous light
> Smothers out sight,
> Surges billowing up, parts—!
> To come rolling in again—starts
> The wheel once more, a renewed weight.

But he—high, slow, heavy of gait
Sees![18]

This dramatization of the "fixed" doggedness that "Sees!" is akin to Whistler's focus upon a central governing principle to provide "harmony" to the particulars of a composition. It is not a feeling, but a controlling strategy—the kind of "key" for which, Pound was arguing in 1909, one had to be "educated up," and through which such painters as Whistler and Turner were allowing one to "see beauty in mists, shadows, a hundred places where you never dreamed of seeing it before."[19]

This "fixed" controlling principle that creates pattern out of the chaos of particulars often appears in Williams's subsequent verse linked to music, painting, or a beckoning woman. Often—as in "From 'The Birth of Venus' Song"—all three motifs operate simultaneously. This poem begins the group of seven that Pound introduced in *The Poetry Review* of October 1912—Williams's first magazine publication. (Although titled "A Selection from *The Tempers*," two of the seven did not appear in Williams's 1913 volume.) Williams alludes to Botticelli's famous *The Birth of Venus* in both poetry and prose for the next fifty years, but this early poem seems to conflate that painting and the same artist's *Primavera*. (Williams would have seen both works at the Uffizi Gallery, Florence).

Come with us and play!
See, we have breasts as women!
From your tents by the sea
Come play with us; it is forbidden!

Come with us and play!
Lo, bare, straight legs in the water!
By our boats we stay
Then swimming away
Come to us; it is forbidden!

Come with us and play!
See, we are tall as women!
Our eyes are keen;
Our hair is bright;
Our voices speak outright;
We revel in the sea's green!
Come play;
It is forbidden![20]

(*CEP*, 20)

The reference to "the sea" invokes *The Birth of Venus,* but the plurality of voices suggests the Venus and her accompanying Graces of *Pri-*

mavera. The latter painting is set in the garden of Venus—in classical myth the Garden of Hesperides—with the Graces at "play," dancing together. The garden grew golden apples, guarded by the daughters of Atlas and also by a dragon, and is thus "forbidden." In the garden of Venus it is eternal Spring—Williams' immutable world again—but this is now a more alien world for the poet than in the 1909 *Poems*. It is a world reserved for the gods. Mercury plucks one of the apples, and Zephyr is emerging from the trees to seize the nymph Chloris. Venus and her Graces beckon from "the sea's green," the color of Williams's "reality" matching the color of garden and sea in each painting. *The Birth of Venus* allusion links the sea to the female and to fertility, the invitation becoming the "song" that produces and controls the poem. But the male poet's discipline—he is addressed as if part of a military encampment—will be overcome by this sea if he succumbs to the invitation. (It is pertinent to Williams's poem that Venus' birth arose from the castration of Uranus.) "It is forbidden" for the poet to accept the invitation not only because this is the realm of the gods, and he risks castration, but also because the vicissitudes of the modern world separate man from the ideal—here the ideal as woman. The invitation is that of a siren voice, compelling and fraught with danger. The poem dramatizes the greatest tension yet in this early work between the ideal and the limitations of contemporary possibility.

The idealized past *has* found voice, however, through the modern poet's "song"—even if he is obliged to acknowledge his distance from its originating impulse and serve merely as the means through which it achieves expression. Williams had clearly responded to the tone of such Pound poems as "The Picture," "Of Jacopo Del Sellaio" (both on Sellaio's painting *Venus Reclining*) and "Histrion".

The Picture

The eyes of this dead lady speak to me,
For here was love, was not to be drowned out,
And here desire, not to be kissed away.

The eyes of this dead lady speak to me.

Of Jacopo Del Sellaio

This man knew out the secret ways of love,
No man could paint such things who did not know.

And now she's gone, who was his Cyprian,
And you are here, who are "The Isles" to me.

And here's the thing that lasts the whole thing out:
The eyes of this dead lady speak to me.

No man hath dared to write this thing as yet,
And yet I know, how that the souls of all men great
At times pass through us,
And we are melted into them, and are not
Save reflexions of their souls. . . .
. . . .
So cease we from all being for the time,
And these, the Masters of the Soul, live on.[21]
                                        (From "Histrion")

In "A Man to a Woman," another poem from Williams's *Poetry Review* series, he acknowledges his inability to build such timeless monuments as the Botticelli painting, but allows for the kind of transmigration declared in "Histrion."

Though you complain of me
    That I build no marvel to your name;
That I have never grappled time to proclaim
    You everlastingly;

Though no marble, however white it be,
    Compels me to win your fame:
My soul is shapen as by a flame
    In your identity.[22]

"From 'The Birth of Venus' Song"—like Pound's similar poems— identifies the haunting, powerful achievements of the past with southern Europe.[23] In Williams's "Homage"—also in the *Poetry Review* series— we find another idealized Latin woman, "Elvira," serving as icon to entice a procession of admirers.

The loud clangor of pretenders
Melteth before you
Like the roll of carts passing,
But you come silently
And homage is given. (*CEP,* 18)[23]

Through "love's grace" Elvira emits "A clear radiance"—her bright southern light contrasting with what another poem in the series, "An After Song," terms "the modern twilight."

In another poem in the group "In San Marco, Venizia," the poet is "an outcast" before "the dream"—here embodied in Renaissance music and architecture.

I for whom the world is a clear stream
Of Beauty's holding,—fashioned to reflect
Her loveliness; a hollow cave perfect
In echo, that her voice meet full esteem,

Around me here are arching walls gold-decked,
Of her grey children breathing forth their praise,
I am an outcast, too strange to but raise
One least harmonious whisper of respect.

I am wild, uncouth; before the dream
Thou givest me I stand weak in amaze,
Or dare I lift one hand to serve, it lays
All waste the very mesh I hold supreme.[24]

In the 1909 *Poems* and in "Min Schleppner" Williams felt the possibility of both seeing and capturing in his verse an idyllic, immutable world. But by 1912 this confidence had become an unfulfilled yearning, which through its lack of permanent consummation shapes the modern identity of poet and poem. The overall strategy has not changed—it is still necessary that the distracting particular be incorporated into a larger "reality"—but that "reality" is now a tradition of achievement that intimidates and overwhelms the modern poet's confidence in his contemporary expression.

Within the next two years, the sense of helplessness before the achievements of the past that pervades such poems as "From 'The Birth of Venus' Song" disappears. In *The Wanderer,* instead of the timeless garden of Venus or the castrating sea, the poet is offered a descent into his own "Passaic, that filthy river"(*CEP,* 11), a stone's throw from Rutherford. The renewed self that emerges from the descent into the river absorbs into its contemporary identity the duality of particular and general represented by the river (local but also the symbol of timelessness), the poem's female guide. (Williams's grandmother but also a mythic prophetess), and the poem itself—a contemporary expression of a continuing tradition.

In *Spring and All, Paterson,* and *In the American Grain*—to cite three major examples—the courage of accepting the invitation to descend into the sea is rewarded, upon the return to shore, by an all-encompassing experience of the full impact of the contemporary, living moment.[25] Williams's subsequent poetry is thus characterized by a creative tension born of accepting the *simultaneous* presence of the particular and the general in the poem. In "Song," (1962), from *Pictures From Brueghel,* a late "Venus" poem, painting, music, and sexual yearning unite in the rooted moment that produces the poem.

beauty is a shell
from the sea
where she rules triumphant
till love has had its way with her

scallops and
lion's paws
sculptured to the
tune of retreating waves

undying accents
repeated till
the ear and the eye lie
down together in the same bed
(*PB*, 15)

In "Song" the constructed poem achieves the immutable reconciliation of particulars that the 1909 *Poems* had reserved for an idealistic "reality," and the 1910–12 verses had conceded to an earlier age. The emphasis, in this late poem, is upon the relevance of the past to the contemporary. But Williams's first struggle, in the years after 1912, was to accept the relevance of the contemporary alongside the achievements of the past—to acknowledge the contemporary particular as a valid source of art, and to accept the patterned presentation of those particulars in a modern poem as a valid form of expression. As Pound was helping him discover, in this struggle the modernist painters had already developed a number of fruitful strategies.

Hilda Doolittle remembered Pound before he set off for Europe in 1908 as "a composite James McNeill Whistler, Peer Gynt, and the victorious and defeated heroes of the William Morris poems and stories." She recalled, "he brought me Whistler's 'Ten O'Clock,' " and "scratched a gadfly, in imitation of Whistler's butterfly, as a sort of signature in his books at that time."[26]

Although it was the Pre-Raphaelite rather than the Whistlerian element in this "composite" that governed many of the sentiments in Pound's earliest verse, by 1909 he was using Whistler's compositional "harmonies" to show a contrast with the Pre-Raphaelites. Defending *A Lume Spento* from Williams's charge of "poetic anarchy," he doubted whether his friend was "sufficiently au courant to know just what the poets and musicians *and* painters are doing with a good deal of convention that has masqueraded as law" (Pound's emphasis).[27] In his 1910 *The Spirit of Romance,* contrasting the Pre-Raphaelite Burne-Jones with Whistler, he argued for "two kinds of beautiful painting—works of art which are beautiful objects and works of art which are keys or passwords admitting one to a deeper knowledge."[28]

The musical association of the term 'key' is significant, and reflects Pound's crucial meeting in London with the incipient imagist group. A central figure in this group, T. E. Hulme, declared in his "Lecture on Modern Poetry" (delivered in 1908 or 9) that the modern experience of "the mystery of things" is "no longer directly in the form of action, but as an impression, for example Whistler's pictures." This "Impressionism" in painting "will soon find expression in poetry as free verse." If the poet is "moved" by a scene, "he selects from that certain images which, put into juxtaposition in separate lines, serve to suggest and evoke the state he feels." The poet creates a "harmony" much like a musician or painter.[29]

Pound was less concerned with the poet's being "moved" than with the discovery of fresh compositional possibilities. Through Hulme and Whistler he discovered that an art could obey formal imperatives geared to its own materials—ignoring the aesthetic expectations of an audience that would confine the artist to the comfortably familiar.

Pound's 1912 poem "To Whistler, American" praises the painter as much for his unceasing experimentation as for his particular achievements. Sending the poem to Harriet Monroe in Chicago for the first issue of her *Poetry* magazine, he told her, "I count him our only great artist, and even this informal salute, drastic as it is, may not be out of place at the threshold of what I hope is an endeavor to carry into our American poetry the same sort of life and intensity which he infused into modern painting."[30]

This approval of Whistler's commitment to formal experimentation is praise one would expect from a poet whose own volumes were studies in a variety of alternative verse structures. It was with the same kind of praise that Pound introduced Williams's poems in the *Poetry Review*. Whistler had taken control of the possibilities of his art—"Had tried all ways; / Tested and pried and worked in many fashions. . . . Had not one style from birth, but tried and pried / And stretched and tampered with the media." Williams too "is not overcrowded with false ornament. He seems to have found his art very difficult and to be possessed of some sort of determination which has carried him through certain impasses."[31]

Apart from Whistler's exploration of the formal properties of his art, a number of other mutual interests attracted Pound to the painter in these early years. Whistler was a fellow expatriate, one who sought international standards of excellence and won international fame—including the approval of Mallarmé, who translated the *Ten O'Clock* lecture. "What Whistler has proved once and for all," Pound declared, "is that being born an American does not eternally damn a man or prevent him from the ultimate and highest achievement in the arts."[32] Whistler's infamous self-promotion was matched by Pound's tireless efforts to advertise both himself and the fellow artists he regarded as unfairly neglected. And both men shared the view that art of the highest standards could not afford to make concessions to its audience—only an elite, educated minority could appreciate its achievement. Whistler's *The Gentle Art of Making Enemies* is uncompromisingly dedicated to "the rare Few, who, early in Life, have rid Themselves of the Friendship of the Many."

Whistler and Pound also shared a similar sense of the place of their innovations in the overall tradition. Whistler, generally credited with revealing the artistic significance of the Japanese print to his English colleagues, told his biographers the Pennells that, "for him, the Japanese influence meant the maintenance of a tradition, and not a revolution, in European art."[33] Pound, and later T. S. Eliot, were equally concerned with placing their modernist innovations within a continuing tradition.

After 1862, with *Symphony in White No. 1,* Whistler gave musical titles to his paintings to emphasize that the various shades of color used were related harmoniously to one another and referred to a central principle. Pound's "Albatre" (1914) juxtaposes two "contrasts in whiteness" to create the kind of "harmony" that Hulme compared to "Whistler's pictures".

> This lady in the white bath-robe which she calls a peignoir,
> Is, for the time being, the mistress of my friend,
> And the delicate white feet of her little white dog
> Are not more delicate than she is,
> Nor would Gautier himself have despised their contrasts in whiteness
> As she sits in the great chair
> Between the two indolent candles.

Whistler's interest in the relationships between painting and music became a common concern in the following decades. As well as Whistler, the painters Marsden Hartley, Gauguin, Odilon Redon, František Kupka, Robert Delaunay and Kandinsky all saw affinities between their work and music. Hulme claimed formal parallels between music and free verse in his "Lecture on Modern Poetry"; Pound followed—but with his own emphasis. Stressing the importance of the French Troubador tradition of the eleventh through thirteenth centuries, he sought to bring out the "song" behind the poem (but with the focus upon parallels of technique, rather than the emotional parallels which interested the symbolist poets). His experiments with medieval verse forms stressed the craftsmanship behind both the structural and the lyrical elements of the composition—and the status of the poem as a pattern of words.

Pound initially shared something of Whistler's attitude toward the modern art movements in Paris too. After the 1870s Whistler rejected the French innovations, and was no admirer of Cézanne. Pound's ambivalence concerning the painters' modernist experiments in Paris lasted until the early 1920s, with his flirtation with Dada, and it is only then that his letters contain unconditional praise of such painters as Duchamp and Picabia.

Before his first trip to Europe in 1908, Pound had encountered a number of minor American painters. Among these were William Brooke Smith, to whom *A Lume Spento* is dedicated, Fred Reed Whiteside in Philadelphia, and Fred Nelson Vance in Crawfordsville, Indiana. When he returned to the United States for seven months in June 1910, his painter associates in New York were Carlton Gliddens, Warren Dahler, and Yeats's father Jack B. Yeats.[34] He seems to have been unaware of Alfred Stieglitz's "291" gallery, or of the pioneer articles and reproductions appearing in Stieglitz's magazine *Camera Work*. Writing in the 1930s, he unfairly remembered New York as maintaining "the London nineties" until 1915. That was the year that Stieglitz sent him copies of *Camera Work* and *291* at the instigation of Alfred Kreymborg, but Pound was undoubtedly remembering his first correspondence with John Quinn over Wyndham Lewis and Gaudier-Brzeska.[35]

Writing from New York in 1911, he told his parents to "read 'The New Art in Paris' in the February *Forum*. There's an answer to a number of things. That ought to prove my instinct for where I can breathe. It's mostly news to me, but of the right sort."[36] The article was by Stieglitz's associate Marius De Zayas. De Zayas praises the receptivity of the Parisian audience to art which it does not initially understand—an atmosphere Pound would certainly appreciate. But the "news" lay in De Zayas's account of the new paintings at the Salon d' Automne. Pound's return to the United States had caused him to miss the November 1910 post-impressionist exhibition held in London's Grafton Galleries.

Among the paintings at the Salon d' Automne were some works of analytical cubism, described by De Zayas as "a multitude of geometrical figures, curves, triangles, ellipses, squares, rhombs." He noted the interest of the movement in primitive art, the artists considering it "less conventional" and "more spontaneous" than art of the present day. He explained that "the movement . . . does not limit itself to painting and the other plastic arts, but extends itself to literature and music," and described attending a poetry reading at the Salon. The poets "make music with words, and we shall see later that the musicians endeavor to play words with harmony."[37] All this would certainly be "news . . . of the right sort" to the poet of Troubadors and the admirer of Whistler.

By the next month Pound was in Paris and could see for himself. He told his mother that he had visited the studio of a "brand new painter," and that he had "seen a number of Cézanne pictures in a private gallery." He visited the Salon Des Independents, declaring "Matisse's one canvas is well painted," although "freaks there are in abundance."[38] The note of skepticism is sounded again in his late 1911 essay series "I Gather the Limbs of Osiris." There he found the contemporary arts "damned and clogged by the mimetic," noting that many of "the painters of the moment escape through eccentricity."[39] When Pound did shortly endorse the productions of the modernist painters, he followed Wyndham Lewis in concentrating upon German ideas rather than the French developments. Lewis announced in *Blast* that it was "unofficial Germany" that "has done more for the movement that this paper was founded to propagate, and for all branches of contemporary activity in Science and Art, than any other country."[40]

2

Al Que Quiere! (1)

In his famous 1913 essay "A Few Don'ts by an Imagiste" Pound defined an "Image" as "that which presents an intellectual and emotional complex in an instant of time."[1] Whistler's pictures invited apprehension in a single instant in terms of the artist's imposition of form, and the imagist poem offered the poet one way to write such a "complex." Through control of form, painting or poetry could manifest a way of seeing—recording the conscious purpose of the artist, and not his enslavement to traditional modes of expression. Throughout his subsequent campaign for "direct treatment of the thing,"[2] and against excess verbiage and mechanical rhythm, Pound continued to espouse Whistler as a forerunner in the contemporary battle. But by 1918 it was not the Whistler revealing secrets in mists and fogs that he praised, but the late etchings, their "clear, hard, definite, one might almost say Meryon manner."[3] The stress is upon the artist's clarity, not so much upon his revelation or evocation of mysteries, and this is akin to the changes Pound wrought in his own work from 1913 on. Such a change informs the progression of his "Xenia" sequence (*Poetry,* Nov. 1913) from its opening "Out of the overhanging gray mist," to the concluding invocation to its own language, "Clear speakers, naked in the sun, untrammelled."[4] The poems of "Contemporania" (April 1913) "without quaint devices . . . with nothing archaic about them" ("Salutation the Second") break up traditional poetic form and clichéd expression of emotion, allowing the voice of indignation full rein. The result is the co-existence of impulse with a precise arrangement that proclaims the poet's right to control the expression of his emotion through the materials of his art. The patterned words within the poem become like the colors and lines in Whistler's "arrangements," "no part but a whole / No portion but a being" ("Ortus").

Reviewing Williams's second published volume, *The Tempers,* in the London journal *The New Freewoman* in December 1913, Pound read his friend as engaged in a similar strategy. Williams "makes a bold attempt to express himself directly and convinces one that the emotions he feels are veritably his own." He noted "the effect of color . . . the particularly vivid and rich range of colour in which his emotions seem to present themselves, 'gold against blue,' to his vision."[5] For Pound, the impulse behind Williams's work is an emotion apprehended visually.

In this same year Pound discussed the germination of his "In a Station of the Metro" (the concluding poem of the "Contemporania" series).

> The apparition of these faces in the crowd;
> Petals on a wet, black bough.

For this account, in *T.P.'s Weekly,* the poem is related to Japanese tradition, "where a work of art is not estimated by its acreage."[6] But a year later his description of translating a pattern of color into a verbal image is retold around a critical apparatus a good deal more painterly. In the later version, titled "Vorticism," he included "Kandinsky and some cubists," along with Whistler, as examples of painters "set to getting extraneous matter out of their art . . . ousting literary values." Together with musicians "the painters realize that what matters is form and colour. . . . The painter should use his colour because he sees it or feels it. . . . It is the same in writing poems, the author must use his *image* because he sees it or feels it." Although the emotion originally appeared to him in terms of a pattern of color, being a poet, not a painter, he sought an "image" to express that emotion where a painter would have recorded the colors. "The image is the poet's pigment; with that in mind you can go ahead and apply Kandinsky, you can transpose his chapter on the language of form and colour and apply it to the writing of verse."[7] (Pound's correspondence with Harriet Monroe on the spacing of the poem in *Poetry* reveals his concern that the visual dimension of the lines be retained in the arrangement of the words on the page.)

Kandinsky's "chapter on the language of form and colour" (from his *Ueber das Geistige in der Kunst,* 1912) was translated and summarized for the first issue of *Blast* (June 1914) by the vorticist painter Edward Wadsworth. Kandinsky's ideas were attractive to Pound, for they offered a strategy to balance individual expression with "the pure and eternal qualities of the art of all men," via the artist's expression of "what is particular to this epoch." In pursuing his argument in this chapter, Kandinsky analyses the particular qualities of various individual colors and shapes, asserting that these colors and shapes are the basic units of composition. The artist must be sensitive to their qualities, and also to the effects possible within the multifold combinations of the basic units. The artist expresses his "inner necessity" by being aware of the "necessities" within himself, his age, and the properties of his art. According to Kandinsky, it is the preponderance of the "pure and eternal qualities" in a work of art that determines its greatness, and allows it to have relevance beyond its own age and its individual creator. Thus "an Egyptian statue astounds us certainly more today than it could have astounded its contemporaries," for such "eternal" qualities are now more clearly visible.[8] Pound discovered in Kandinsky's ideas a way to move beyond the kind of transmigration of "souls" recorded in "Of Jacopo Del Sellaio" and "Histrion," towards a strategy that allowed past models of achievement to resonate within uncompromisingly contemporary expression. The German expressionists' *Bleue Reiter Almanac* (1912), edited by Kandinsky and Franz Marc, carried illustrations of art from many cultures and centuries as well as reproductions of work from their own school. Their view matched Pound's in 1914 that "the first step of a renaissance, or awakening, is the importation of models for painting, sculpture or writing."[9] In *The Egoist* Pound discussed the Assyrian archeological discoveries, (which also interested Williams and Gaudier-Brzeska). "It was better to dig up the bas-reliefs of Assurbanipal's hunting than to have done an equal amount of Royal Academy sculpture. There are times when archeology is almost equal to creation, or when a resurrection is equally creative or even more creative than invention."[10] The Italian futurists, on the other hand, whose views Marinetti was tirelessly expounding in London at this time, denied any relevance to the past in their call for contemporary expression.

Although Pound encountered Kandinsky's theories through his association with the vorticist group of painters, writers and sculptors, not all the figures in that movement held the painter in high regard. Wadsworth introduced his translation in *Blast* by describing Kandinsky's ideas as "a most important contribution to the psychology of modern art," but Gaudier-Brzeska dismissed the painter's work as "formless, vague assertions."[11] For Wyndham Lewis, Kandinsky's canvases lacked the definiteness of line that characterized vorticist productions: his work was "ethereal, lyrical, and cloud-like," while his theory committed him "to avoid almost all powerful and definite forms."[12]

By January 1915 Pound himself was prepared to concede that Lewis might be "a more significant artist than Kandinsky."[13] But whatever his reservations about Kandinsky's work (of which he had probably seen little), he was clearly attracted to a theory which so paralleled his own practice, and it was an attraction that Williams shared. If form and color have their own "reality," through which the artist can express his emotional impetus—his composition shaped by the pressure of his own time and the intrinsic qualities of his particular art form—it follows that art need not limit itself to forms based upon accumulated conventions. Poetry need not confine itself to traditional modes of organization—rhyme, narrative, meter—or to conventional subjects, or to a use of "poetic" language. Form was constructed from a meeting between the intrinsic qualities informing the individual elements of an art form, and the artist's realization of his emotions through an arrangement of those elements. For Kandinsky, this justified abstract art, for the more abstract the form "the more purely and therefore the more primitively it will resound." For Pound, and even more for Williams as he continued to explore the implications of this strategy, it redefined the nature of tradition, and it justified the view of a poem as a unique, self-referential word construction.

While Kandinsky's ideas play an important part in Pound's thought at this time, his writing also reflects an awareness of the ideas of Wilhelm Worringer. It was probably Worringer that Lewis had in mind when he wrote of the "unofficial Germany"[14] behind many of the ideas in *Blast*. Worringer, writing three or four years before Kandinsky, provided an important rationale for the new abstract art by placing it in the context of the history of art in general. Franz Marc praised his *Abstraktion und Einfuhlung* (1908) as one of the two important attempts to create a basis for a new criticism in art (the other being Kandinsky's book).[15] Worringer's contribution was to argue that differences in the kinds of art produced in different cultures through the ages were the result, not of different abilities in the artists, but of differences in artistic intent. These intentions were the result of the varying needs which art fulfilled for different ages, different races, and different geographical regions. Worringer's ideas were introduced to Pound, and to England, by T. E. Hulme.

Pound wrote to his mother on 20 January 1914, "Hulme lectured at the QUEST last night on futurism and post-impressionism, followed by fervent harangues from Wyndham Lewis and myself."[16] What Hulme actually lectured on was Worringer's aesthetics. His talk survives as "Modern Art and its Philosophy" collected in *Speculations*, much of the argument, as he confesses, "practically an abstract of Worringer's views."[17]

As Hulme repeats, Worringer's concern in *Abstraktion und Einfuhlung* was to examine the social needs that determined whether the art of a particular age was manifest in representational or nonrepresentational terms. There are two kinds of art, "vital" and "geometrical," these being "absolutely distinct in kind from one another." Each kind of art "springs from and corresponds to a certain general attitude towards the world." "Vital" art—exemplified by the Greeks and humanistic art since the Renaissance—"can be broadly described as naturalism or realism." It occurs when a people feel comfort and pleasure in the contemplation of "forms and movements to be found in nature." "Geometrical" art—found in primitive peoples, in Egyptian, Byzantine, and contemporary art—occurs when a people has "a feeling of separation in the face of outside nature." The abstraction results from "a desire to create a certain abstract geometrical shape, which, being durable and permanent, shall be a refuge from the flux and impermanence of outside nature." Taking up Worringer's idea that the disjunction of the consciousness of a people with outside nature is caused by different factors in different societies, and that consequently each manifestation of geometrical art is unique, Hulme posits the possible characteristics of the coming geometrical art. Not surprisingly, these conform to the characteristics of vorticism. The new art will have a parallel in "the idea of machinery . . . having an organization, and governed by principles, which are at present exemplified unintentionally, as it were, in machinery." But despite the uniqueness of each geometrical style, each new style evolves from an initial return to previous geometrical models. Futurism rejected all of the past, and for this reason earns Hulme's scorn—as it earned the scorn of Pound and Lewis. The analytical cubists are a little less in error, but they fail to transform their theories into "a constructive geometrical art." Hulme concludes that the most significant modern artists are the vorticists Wyndham Lewis and Jacob Epstein.[18]

Pound reported on the Quest meeting for *Egoist* readers on 16 February 1914, and summarized a number of Hulme's points. He describes Hulme's lecture as "almost wholly unintelligible," but this is sarcasm directed at the audience, not Hulme. Pound clearly found it intelligible, and concludes "Mr. Hulme was quite right in saying that the difference between the new art and the old was not a difference in degree but a difference in kind; a difference in intention." He echoes Hulme's choice of artists, "Epstein is the only sculptor in England" (although he finds Gaudier-Brzeska also worthy of note). And he adopts Worringer's framework to assert that "these men work in an unchanging world."

Pound's own talk—described in his report as given by "a third speaker"—discusses the "two totally opposed theories of aesthetic" that come from either regarding art as passive acceptance of sensations, or "as an instrument for carrying out the decrees of the will (or the soul)"— Kandinsky's word—"or whatever you wish to term it." This art of the "will" is essentially undemocratic, the artist taking no more heed of "general franchise" than he does of conventional form.[19]

In the correspondence columns of *The Egoist* Pound subsequently defended his attack upon Greek art (art produced through empathy with outside nature for Worringer, Hulme, and Gaudier-Brzeska). The modern artist, he explained, does not consider "BEAUTIFUL" only "the caressable, the physically attractive." He takes a broader perspective, and relates his art to "other masterpieces from Egypt and from India and from China."[20]

Pound continued this approach to modern art in subsequent *Egoist* essays, such as those on Lewis (June 1914) and Wadsworth (August 1914). In the latter piece he sees Wadsworth as continuing the tradition of "Whistler and the Japanese," expressing himself through "arrangements of colours and masses," in an art akin to "notes in a fugue."[21] In his "Vortex" manifesto for the first *Blast* he summarized many of his earlier distinctions. The finest art is that which directs "all the energized past" into the contemporary form appropriate for each particular art. Whistler and Kandinsky both appear in the "ancestry" of this "Vortex."[22]

Pound presented the same idea from another perspective in his sculpting analogies. The modern sculptor cuts at the stone and discovers the form within, *not* imposing conventional representations of nature upon his material. The form discovered—as Gaudier-Brzeska's work reveals, and Kandinsky and Worringer's theories assert—is both uniquely modern and suggestive of that "energized past" to which the artist must attune himself as he creates.

This discovery of form is still a "making" of form, and not a passive "finding." In his "Affirmations: Vorticism" essay of January 1915, Pound dismissed "impressions" of color and form, and also "automatic" writing and painting, declaring "this is not vorticism." The forms of vorticism were no kind of Jungean archetypes received passively by the unconscious. Rather, they were constructed out of a conception akin to Worringer's geometrical vision: "conceiving the forms about one as a source of 'form-motifs', which motifs one can use later at one's pleasure in more highly developed compositions."[23]

Gaudier-Brzeska's "Vortex" in the first issue of *Blast* also mirrors Worringer's approach, arguing the history of sculptural form in terms of historical, racial, and climactic necessity. Like Pound, he stressed "will and consciousness" as the force behind the modern vortex.[24] In his own work—such as the *Hieratic Head of Ezra Pound*—the modern geometrical modeling has clear affinities to primitive art. Sometimes, as the title of the head of Pound suggests, the affinity is to Egyptian work, and there is often a sexual dimension to the shape, suggesting the primal creative energies behind all manifestations of form.

For Pound, the modern poet was in a disharmony with his immediate surroundings that made him kin to those artists of past and present whose similar disjunction produced *their* abstract art. This hostile environment often appears in Pound's poems of these years as the philistine literary establishment of editors, academics, and febrile writers who threaten the livelihood and work of the genuine artist. In poems such as "Et Faim Sallir les Loups des Boys" the isolation is presented dramatically.

> I cling to the spar,
> Washed with the cold salt ice
> I cling to the spar—
> Insidious modern waves, civilization,
>   civilized hidden snares.

The 1920 *Hugh Selwyn Mauberley* sequence can be read as two perspectives on the modern poet's challenge. In "Envoi" the poet E. P. tries to translate his feelings into a lyrical form reflecting the "energized past" that will be more durable than the truncated efforts of the Pre-Raphaelites and the nineties generation. But the lyrical achievement, although a triumph, dangerously skirts literary pastiche. Mauberley, however, *does* achieve a durability and permanence in his "Medallion," but at the cost of slipping from "the spar." The "pure and eternal" qualities of art can only be appreciated after the artist's death, and Mauberley's existence is recorded only as an epitaph on an oar.

"Envoi" and "Medallion" correspond to the "two sorts of poetry" Pound distinguished in 1914 as "the most poetic": "they are, firstly, the sort of poetry which seems to be music just forcing itself into articulate speech, and, secondly, that sort of poetry which seems as if sculpture or painting were just forced or forcing itself into words."[25] Both sorts of poetry are "arrangements"; many of Pound's poems reach for the ideal of a lyrical and a sculptural quality together. The poem, composed at the level of individual word and line, builds up its own logic "as in Gaudier's brown stone dancer, the pure or unadulterated motifs of the circle and triangle have a right to build up their own fugue or sonata in form; as a theme in music has a right to express itself."[26]

The idea of a composite form built out of discrete elements is also behind Pound's definition of vorticist poetry as "an image or a procession of images."[27] Critics have often pointed to the frequency of the procession motif in the 1916 *Lustra* poems. A procession not only encapsulates the idea of moments of an "energized past," itself an archetypal form of celebration, it also combines color, music, discipline, and will in an aggregation of elements, each unique and indispensable in the overall pattern.

Pound's critical terms to describe the desired qualities in the new verse stress both the sculptural analogies and the constructive role of the artist. The form should be "hard," "clear," and should cut with an "edge" (the last term one that Williams frequently used). In contrast with these qualities are elements in a work which bear no relation to its intrinsic logic; these elements are "ornament" or "decoration". Or there is the merely sensuous, such as the undisciplined color of "L'Art 1910" which provides merely a "feast" for the "eyes." Just as fallacious is poetry which only copies "what someone has done in paint,"[28] for that denies the careful attention necessary to the demands of the writer's own art form. The ideal is that balance captured in the phrase "just forced or forcing itself." Beauty is arrangement, not description, as "the young Dante" of "The Study in Aesthetics" knows as he strokes "the fish in the boxes." It is something beyond the "inexplicable correlations" of "the elderly mind"—"small dogs and the young" can see minutely because they are not beset with such habitual connections ("The Seeing Eye").[29]

The "vortex" ideal is the expression of contemporary emotion translated through close attention to the universal qualities of form. Pound's most clearly vorticist poem, "The Game of Chess," locks its verbs of movement within a metaphor of shapes and patterns which have their own delimited volition.

> Red knights, brown bishops, bright queens,
> Striking the board, falling in strong "L"'s of
>   colour.
> Reaching and striking in angles,
>   holding lines in one colour.
> This board is alive with light;
>   these pieces are living in form,
> Their moves break and reform the pattern:
>   luminous green from the rooks,
> Clashing with "X"'s of queens,
>   looped with the knight-leaps.
>
> "Y" pawns, cleaving, embanking!
> Whirl! Centripetal! Mate! King down in the
>   vortex,
> Clash, leaping of bands, straight strips of hard
>   colour,
> Blocked lights working in. Escapes. Renewal of
>   contest.

Each separate arrangement of pieces on the checkered board is a manifestation of "living in form," and within the geometrical constraints the variations are manifold. This poem is appropriately subtitled, "Dogmatic Statement Concerning the Game of Chess: Theme for a Series of Pictures."

Williams followed this ferment of ideas in London as he moved towards his poetic independence with the New York/New Jersey "Others" group. In 1912 Pound sent him the new Chicago *Poetry,* advising him to subscribe, and in the same year dedicated the volume *Ripostes* to him. In 1913 he arranged for the publication of Williams's *The Tempers* with Elkin Matthews in London. Writing to Williams at the end of this year, he told him to subscribe to *The Egoist* and to watch out for "*the* coming sculptor, Gaudier-Brzeska."[30] He included Williams in the imagist anthologies *Des Imagistes* (1914) and *Catholic Anthology* (1915).

In *Poetry* and *The Egoist* Williams followed the outpourings of imagist verse and critiques, telling his friend Viola Jordan in June 1914 that he was himself an imagist, and that she was underestimating the worth of *The Egoist*. In telling her to read that month's *Poetry* for Ford Maddox Ford's "On Heaven" he implied his agreement with the view of Pound and Richard Aldington that the work was the finest yet to emerge from the new movement.[31]

When Pound moved from imagism to vorticism, making imagism, according to F. S. Flint, "to mean pictures as Wyndham Lewis understands them,"[32] Williams responded with similar experiments. His poems in *The Tempers* follow Pound in evincing a nostalgia for past eras when the importance of poetry was clearly manifest, but as Pound developed a strategy for bringing the "energized past" to bear upon the concerns of the modern poet, so the note of nostalgia disappears in Williams's work. A number of his poems from these years demonstrate this interest in the cycles of art as they are discussed in the work of Pound, Hulme, and Gaudier-Brzeska. Past models of geometrical art are brought into poems that map out a strategy for the contemporary expression of the poet's America.

Vorticism now receives little space in histories of modern painting—its contribution is seen as local and far less important than the innovations of Paris and Berlin. But Pound characteristically made sure that the movement was publicized in his home country. In New York, John Quinn purchased a number of Gaudier-Brzeska's pieces, and Quinn and Pound arranged a three week vorticist exhibition at the Penguin Club for January 1917. The show included forty-five works by Wyndham Lewis, and was publicized by the mailing of two thousand publicity postcards. *The New York Times* reported that at the opening party a number of American vorticists were in attendance.[33]

Evidence of interest in vorticism among the "Others" group comes not only from Williams's verse, and his 1915 "Vortex" essay, but also from Pound's letter to his father of October 1915. He asks for that month's *Current Opinion*, in which "Kreymborg writes me that there is something about Gaudier and myself." (The magazine reproduced Gaudier's *Hieratic Head of Ezra Pound*, and printed some of his "Vortex" from the second *Blast*.)[34] The group could also read Pound's memoir of the sculptor, which contains many of the manifestoes of vorticism, when the book was published in the United States in 1916. (Pound corresponded with Kreymborg into the 1920s, and when he visited Europe in 1922 Pound insisted he meet Lewis in London, adding that they should have met "long ago.")[35]

Williams's "Vortex" essay is a response to Gaudier-Brzeska's "Vortex" from the second and final issue of *Blast*. Gaudier, writing from the French trenches, declared that despite all the destruction and death around him "the small individual" can and must "assert himself" over the ephemera of his surroundings. War does not alter form, "the outlines of the hill we are besieging" remain the same. The sculptor will "derive" his "emotions" not through the passing tragedies of battle, but through "will" and "decision . . . solely from the arrangement of surfaces, I shall present my emotions by the arrangement of my surfaces, the planes and lines by which they are defined."[36]

Williams declares his right to borrow phrases from Gaudier's "Vortex" because it is a conscious, willed application to his own purpose. Such a strategy brings him that stability that Worringer described as the driving motive behind geometrical art: "I deny—(affirm my independence from)—the accident of time and place that brought the particular phrases to me . . . by accepting the opportunity that has best satisfied my desire to express my emotions in the environment in which I have happened to be, I have defied my environment and denied its power to control me." Like Gaudier, he will express his emotion "by an arrangement of appearances (of planes) for by appearances I know my emotion. (I amplify 'planes' to include sounds, smells, colors, touch used as planes in the geometric sense)" (*ARI*, 57–58).

In Williams's 1916 "Danse Russe" (*CEP*, 148) the poet's dance of isolation is expressed through such a series of "planes".

> If when my wife is sleeping
> and the baby and Kathleen
> are sleeping
> and the sun is a flame-white disc
> in silken mists
> above shining trees,—
> if I in my north room
> dance naked, grotesquely
> before my mirror
> waving my shirt round my head
> and singing softly to myself:
> "I am lonely, lonely.
> I was born to be lonely,
> I am best so!"

> If I admire my arms, my face,
> my shoulders, flanks, buttocks
> against the yellow drawn shades,—
>
> Who shall say I am not
> the happy genius of my household?

The outside world is at a remove from the room, and is seen as light against the window shades. The singing poet ("I amplify 'planes' to include sounds"), dancing the dance of the satyr, admires the various facets of his naked body, in the mirror, "against the yellow drawn shades." The two flat surfaces against the planes of the moving body complete the perceptual framework for the poem's concluding affirmation of creative genius.

The poem "Smell!" of 1917 (*CEP*, 153) involves the meaning of "planes" as touch, smell, and shape.

> Oh strong-ridged and deeply hollowed
> nose of mine! what will you not be smelling?
> What tactless asses we are, you and I boney nose
> always indiscriminate, always unashamed,
> and now it is the souring flowers of the bedraggled
> poplars: a festering pulp on the wet earth
> beneath them. With what deep thirst
> we quicken our desires
> to that rank odor of a passing springtime!
> Can you not be decent? Can you not reserve your ardors
> For something less unlovely? What girl will care
> for us, do you think, if we continue in these ways?
> Must you taste everything? Must you know everything?
> Must you have a part in everything?

The nose is "boney," and it is "strong-ridged and deeply hollowed." In indiscriminately touching the "passing springtime" through its sensitivity to smell, it makes the world its own, ignoring conventional dictates of selection. It will "have a part in everything." And by addressing his "nose" as if it were separate from himself, Williams not only achieves a delightful comic effect at the expense of the conventions of poetic evocation, but he emphasizes the final separation of the arrangement of planes (nose itself and smells) from himself. The "nose" has its own "inner necessity," and its expressive planes, like the poem, are ultimately autonomous.

The 1916 "Metric Figure" describes the new movements in art as revelatory of form.

> Veils of clarity
> have succeeded
> veils of color

Color, as Kandinsky argued in his analysis of its effects, should be a directed, knowledgeable application of the primary elements of painterly self-expression. Through the sensitive appreciation of its intrinsic qualities, color is to be utilized as carefully as any other formal element in art. Color is revelatory of form, not bound to conventional representations of nature. In "La Flor" (1914) it is Williams's praise of Pound over "versifiers" that "his verse is crimson when they speak of the rose," and he contrasts Pound with "Those who bring their ingenious tapestries to such soft perfection / Borrowing majesty from a true likeness to natural splendour."[37] In Williams's "Metric Figure,"

> Veils of clarity
> have succeeded
> veils of color
> that wove
> as the sea
> sliding above
> submerged whiteness
>
> Veils of clarity
> reveal sand
> glistening—
> falling away
> to an edge—
> sliding
> beneath the advancing ripples[38]

On one level the poem presents sunrise, but on another it describes the shift from impressionism to the hard-edged geometrics of modernist art. Changes in poetry—from atmospheric verse to the "clarity" of imagism—have accompanied the developments in the visual arts. The "veils of color" that informed impressionist work have given way to the controlling clarity of an art that reveals "an edge." The light and sea are now "advancing" instead of "sliding," while the revealed matter of art falls away towards its expressive angularity—its "edge."

In Williams's *Tempers* poems, the "eternal" qualities of art mourned for being no longer accessible to the modern poet are rooted in such idealistic female figures as Venus, and the 'Elvira' of "Homage." Within Williams's developing strategies for contemporary expression, sexual union becomes one of his frequent metaphors for the modern poet attuning himself to the primal energies in the "energized past." The female is associated with the "eternal" qualities of earth, her spirit forming what Williams called in a letter to *The Egoist* "an unalterable chain, every link of which is concrete." The male psyche, he argued, represents the trend to abstraction. The male "characteristically generalizes" and there is a "universal lack of attachment between the male and an objective world—to the earth under feet."[39]

That stability within the flux which the vorticists—following Worringer—saw geometrical art providing, is represented in Williams's work by the abstract male achieving consummation with the rooted female. The male art becomes itself a reality by being infused with the special qualities of female nature. The union is not a capitulation to that nature, but an infusion of its energies to the poet's own purpose, with the result that the poem achieves a life of its own. This sexual metaphor is another of Williams's versions of Kandinsky's "inner necessity"—the drive that unites the artist's expression and the formal qualities of his art.

Williams's development of this idea in his frequent use of plant and tree motifs is an interesting one, for the motifs provide a visual correspondence to his presentation of art as sexual union. The petals, branches, or twigs as intersecting planes express the male spirit rooted in the sustenance of the female earth. The cover that Williams designed for *Al Que Quiere!* is another visual manifestation of the idea, its five-sided geometrical figure being firmly anchored to a base of solid black line.

In Williams's "A Portrait in Greys," (1917) the skyward moving male spirit of the poem addresses the earthbound female.

> Must I be always
> moving counter to you? Is there no place
> where we can be at peace together
> and the motion of our drawing apart
> be altogether taken up?
>
> (*CEP*, 160)

The poem itself, this Whistlerian-titled portrait of "broken" lines and fertile energy, is the meeting place for the conjunction of forces.

In "January Morning," "March," "Overture to a Dance of Locomotives," and "History," Williams attempts longer poems patterned around the pressure of the "energized past" upon the contemporary poet. As a vorticist poem is "a procession of images," so these longer poems are patterns built of a procession of moments of perception, and moments of past creative insight. The tapped energy of the past propels the poems' apparently disparate elements forward, bringing a climactic pressure upon the poet as he prepares to express the current moment in an equally permanent, "energized" form.

The 1917 "January Morning" (*CEP*, 162–66) is a "suite" of fifteen sections—the sections admitting of various ways of being ordered. They are numbered consecutively I to XV. As narrative, they describe a dawn journey to the ferry and across the Hudson to Manhattan. The poem moves from its "smoky dawn" to "after dark", and to the invocation of roaming, adolescent energies. But dawn itself is "after dark," and the poem invites apprehension of its increment of images in a single, circular instant. On another "plane," the poem posits a line of continuity in American verse from Whitman's "Crossing Brooklyn Ferry." There is also a historical pattern. American art is placed alongside European in the juxtaposition set up between the "Church of / the Paulist Fathers in Weehawken" and "Saint Peters / approached after years of anticipation." The ferryboat is named after Shakespeare's "Arden," but plies the "ever-new river." The weaving of past and present continues as "Touchstone" is imagined at the wheel—the reluctant traveller of *As You Like It* who chanced to find love. The poet conjures "the ghost of the Half-Moon," the ship in which Hudson set out to explore the North West Passage, and instead came upon the river that now bears his name—another discovery made without "anticipation." Hudson abandoned his search at Albany, but "January Morning" asserts that its own "suite" can be completed if—in its final section—the "old woman" will understand the necessity that has dictated its pattern.

> All this—
> was for you, old woman.
> I wanted to write a poem
> that you would understand.
> For what good is it to me
> if you can't understand it?
> But you got to try hard—

The poem's "maleness" has produced its broken sections, its intersecting planes like the "long yellow rushes bending."

> what an angle
> you make with each other as
> you lie there in contemplation

But they demand integration into the female spirit of the "old woman." In its multiple "angles" set against the energies of a primitive female spirit, "January Morning" foreshadows the far more complex patterning of *Spring and All* around the "Arab / Indian / dark woman" of its final poem.

In "January Morning" the male poet's perceptions are new—it is dawn, January—they are attached to no "unalterable chain" as is the female spirit. "At the prow of the ferry" behind his own forward-propelled angle, the poet's vision is 'geometrical' and "broken." An initial form of order—"the tall probationers / in their tan uniforms" and the "neatly coiffed, middle-aged gentlemen / with orderly moustaches and / well-brushed coats"—is broken down as the journey proceeds. Finally the old conventions of order are as "dead" as the "admiral" (the poet at his prow now the leader) for whom "the flapping flags are at / half mast." The poem continues, recording a way of seeing that resists integration into a preconceived pattern: "the irregular red houselets," "a young horse . . . bared teeth and nozzle high in the air!", "a semi-circle of dirt-colored men," "the worn / blue car rails (like the sky!) /gleaming among the cobbles!", and the "long / circlets of silver." While these are a precise description of what the poet sees, they are also elements of pattern, and record his mode of perception, not merely what the journey offers to be seen.

What Williams is attempting here with language parallels an important passage in Kandinsky's chapter "on the language of form and colour" that Pound applied to the writing of verse. Kandinsky discusses the interdependence of forms in a harmony of composition, and especially the interaction of "organic form" copied from nature with "abstract" form. He argues that the relationship of forms is more difficult both for artist and spectator when the composition consists entirely of abstract forms—(in the poem "you got to try hard"). Although "the difficulties of art will increase . . . at the same time the abundance of forms—as a means of expression—will increase also, both in quality and quantity." The way language in "January Morning" is used to describe a mode of perception matches Kandinsky's point that "the question of bad drawing will disappear and will be replaced by another much more aesthetic consideration. How far is the inner Timbre of the given object mystified or defined?" Just as the poem builds up its own patterns "at an angle /. . . with each other," so Kandinsky argues that "the combination of the mysterious and the definite will create a new possibility of Leitmotive in a composition of forms."

"March" (1916) (*CEP,* 43–46) presents the "energized past" captured in two earlier works of art as preliminary to the contemporary poet's own attempt to create such a work. But the earlier works of art are also "planes" of his emotion, and by the end of the poem his own individual personality—his "I"—has become fused with the creative force of the new season: "I spring among them." "Spring" becomes the birth of the contemporary manifestation as well as the timeless renewal of regenerative energies. And this "spring" is effected against a hostile environment.

> a flower or two picked
> from mud or from among wet leaves
> or at best against treacherous
> bitterness of wind, and sky shining
> teasingly, then closing in black
> and sudden, with fierce jaws.

The first example of 'spring's' creation is actually two works—the Assyrian Ashurbanipal lion-hunt reliefs from the British Museum, and the Berlin Museum's glazed brick reliefs of bulls and dragons from Nebuchadnessar's Ishtar gate at Babylon.[40] As noted earlier, the Assyrian reliefs also interested Pound, and elsewhere he refers to Epstein's "Babylonian austerity."[41] Williams's combining the Assyrian lion-hunt reliefs with the Ishtar Gate's "sacred bulls / alternately / in four tiers" mirrors a section of Gaudier-Brzeska's 1914 "Vortex." There, as an example of "The Semetic Vortex . . . the lust of war" he asserts, "From Sargon to Amir-nasipal men built man-headed bulls in horizontal flight walk. Men flayed their captives alive and erected howling lions: THE ELONGATED HORIZONTAL SPHERE BUTTRESSED ON FOUR COLUMNS, and their kingdoms disappeared."[42]

Both kings and both series of reliefs represent a similar aspect of the "energized past." Ashurbanipal and Nebuchadnessar were renowned for their conquests in war, but under both kings art and architecture also flourished notably. Being hunters and warriors, they conform to the "rootless" male Williams described in *The Egoist* as "when not busied with women and when free to perform his own will is either hunting, fighting, loafing, or drunk."[43]

But the spirit that produced this art has infused it with a life that defeats time, a life that can be recognized in an age that shares its concerns. For a world at war, and alive to geometrical expression, "they are coming into bloom again!" And as elsewhere, Williams equates this fertility with sexual energy, for the procession is "marching" towards "the god, Marduk." The chief god of Babylon and Babylonia, Marduk is portrayed in the oldest monuments holding a triangular spade or hoe representing fertility and vegetation. The other god in this section, Ishtar, after whom the gate is named, was appropriately the Assyrian goddess of both love *and* war.

With Fra Angelico's mural *Annunciation* comprising the "second spring," the creative spirit of the poem rests in female guise, "painted a virgin." The subject matter is spiritual, not mimetic, and its "eternal" qualities allow it to defeat time despite being painted on "plaster walls." Williams emphasizes the geometrical outline of the work, the "three-legged stool," the crossed arms, the stillness, and the balance of the two figures in opposition. The formal tension is inherently sexual, while the relationship of the sexual and the creative to hunting continues.

> the angel's eyes
> holding the eyes of Mary
> as a snake's hold a bird's.

The analogy is suitably made through a way of seeing.

The past two springs have provided warmth, but the challenge to: the "lean and frozen" modern poet is to create a similar 'warmth' in his own art. His search takes up the energy of the kings' ("now for the battle") and of the Fra Angelico fresco ("lean, serious as a virgin"). Like Pound's ideal of the poet as sculptor, this unified spirit of spring will "cut savagely!" against the "counter-cutting winds" to find its own "flowers."

> lean, serious as a virgin,
> seeking, seeking the flowers of March.
> Seeking
> flowers nowhere to be found . . .
>
> I deride with all the ridicule
> of misery—
> my own starved misery.
> Counter-cutting winds strike against me
> refreshing their fury!
>
> Come, good, cold fellows!
> Have we no flowers?
> Defy then with even more
> desperation than ever—being
> lean and frozen!
>
> But though you are lean and frozen—
> think of the blue bulls of Babylon.
> Fling yourselves upon
> their empty roses—
> cut savagely!
>
> But—
> think of the painted monastery
> at Fiesole.[44]

Although "Overture to a Dance of Locomotives" (*CEP*, 194–5) first appeared in Williams's 1921 volume *Sour Grapes*, and he remembered that he had read the poem at the 1913 Armory Show, its date of composition is certainly 1916–17. The poem has much in common with "March," "History," and "January Morning." In addition, Williams recalled reading the poem together with "Portrait of a Woman in Bed" at a show where Mina Loy was present and this description fits the 1917 Independents Exhibition. Newspaper advertisements for the show included notice of "free readings by American poets" for Wednesday afternoon, April 18. In fact, "Overture to a Dance of Locomotives" would have been particularly appropriate at the Independents Exhibition, for the show took place at the Grand Central Palace in New York. The building had recently been constructed over the new underground tracks of the rebuilt Grand Central Station.[45]

The station concourse is itself a showcase of art, a "gallery" with a long tradition of ritual and form.

> Men with picked voices chant the names
> of cities in a huge gallery . . .
> A leaning pyramid of sunlight . . .
>   moves by the clock;

The pyramid shape—which also appears in "History" and "March"—moves *beyond* the clock to a moment of the poem's own making, and not "by the clock" which controls the lives of "the shuffling . . . ants."

The geometrical forms of the poem ultimately defeat time in the sureness of their patterned "dance." The cylinder is the "Vortex of Fecundity" for Gaudier-Brzeska,[46] and here "dingy cylinders / packed with a warm glow" are "poised horizontal / on glittering parallels" pulling "against the hour." The ceiling lights "hang crooked." And to a litany of numbers the wheels gather the energy and speed to appear "relatively / stationary" to the onlooker. Like the interlocking forms of a vorticist painting, or the "planes" by which Williams wrote in 1915 that he would know his "emotion," both wheels and rails are locked in a self-referential form that captures both stillness and energy.

> wheels repeating
> the same gesture remain relatively
> stationary: rails forever parallel
> return on themselves infinitely.
>   The dance is sure.

"History" (*CEP*, 49–53) first appeared in *Poetry* in July 1917 heavily censored by the editor Harriet Monroe. In its *Al Que Quiere!* and subsequent printings it begins—as does "March"—with reference to "the pyramids." Gaudier-Brzeska titled this shape "the HAMITE VORTEX," associating it with "religion and divinity," while Kandinsky devoted a chapter to "The Pyramid," declaring: "Every man who steeps himself in the spiritual possibilities of his art is a valuable helper in the building of the spiritual pyramid which will some day reach to heaven."[47] Both associations are appropriate to "March" and "History" because of the spiritual quality resonant in their examples of past art. Religious models once had efficacy, but on "History['s]" modern "Sunday, day of worship" a contemporary power must be found against the ravages of time and death. The "wind" which "might blow a lotus petal / over the pyramids" is "not this wind." A visit to a museum may provide an insight into an earlier satisfaction of the need, but finally the contemporary demand must be satisfied on its own terms.

The central sections of the poem dramatize the defeat of time and decay through the power of love and the skill of the craftsman.

> "The chisel is in your hand, the block
> is before you, cut as I shall dictate:
> This is the coffin of Uresh-Nai,
> priest to the Sky Goddess,—built
> to endure forever!

The original printing in *Poetry* and *Al Que Quiere!* of "priestess" for "priest" confused the sexual theme of the poem. Again male love of the female (here for the sky goddess Mut) is expressed in art, an art made timeless through creativity controlled by a fusion of that love with the male dictates of the creator. "The priest has passed into his tomb," but "the stone has taken up his spirit." This spirit can speak to the modern artist of its endurance, of how its "granite holds an edge against / the weather." "This / northern scenery is not the Nile," yet history lives on outside the museum in the races that compose America, and its "young" world demands enduring expression from its artists.

> But it is five o'clock. Come!
> Life is good—enjoy it!
> A walk in the park while the day lasts.
> I will go with you. Look! this
> northern scenery is not the Nile, but—
> these benches—the yellow and purple
>   dusk—
> the moon there—these tired people—
> the lights on the water!
>
> Are not these Jews and—Ethiopians?
> The world is young, surely! Young

                    and colored like—a girl that has come
                         upon
                    a lover! Will that do?

Williams chose not to reprint this poem until 1951, and he commented in the 1950s on how "studied" the poem later appeared to him: "I was self-consciously talking about history and it showed" (*IWWP,* 25). It is "studied" in that it proposes but does not fulfill the demand Williams began to make of himself to express American consciousness through a distinctively American poem. However "History" did provide him with a title in 1939 for "Against the Weather," one of his most important essays on the challenge facing the American artist (perhaps from rereading the poem the previous year for possible inclusion in the 1938 *Collected Poems*). His definition there of a work of art could apply to the strategy behind these earlier poems.

> A life that is here and now is timeless. That is the universal I am seeking: to embody that in a work of art, a new world that is always "real."
> All things otherwise grow old and rot. By long experience the only thing that remains unchanged and unchangeable is the work of art. It is because of the element of timelessness in it, its sensuality. The only world that exists is the world of the senses. The world of the artist. (*SE,* 196)

Although the strategy does not change, Williams continued to experiment with its implications, especially the double meaning of "a new world" as American experience and modern poem. Worringer and Kandinsky offered one way to combine "sensuality" and "timelessness," and Williams explored this further in his prose Improvisations for *Kora in Hell.* But by 1923, the year of *Spring and All,* expressionism and Kandinsky were both dismissed as appropriate only to "the seething reactions of the contemporary European consciousness" (*Imag,* 173). Pound had directed Williams to the ideas coming out of that "contemporary European consciousness," but now Williams had to place an American stamp upon those ideas. In meeting the "Others" group, and Marsden Hartley, in the years after 1914, he joined other American artists similarly groping both for an individual and a national voice within the international upheaval in the arts.

3

Al Que Quiere! (2)

Williams's contacts with the New York avant-garde increased considerably in the years between *The Tempers* and *Al Que Quiere!*. Avant-garde activity in New York, like that in London and Paris, was centered on the new developments in the visual arts. In a 1916 letter to *The Egoist*, Williams mentions "an exhibition of Cézanne at Knoedler's and one of young Americans, the Forum Exhibit," as examples of the artistic "quickening" in New York (*SL*, 30). (Although, with the former, Williams was probably remembering the Cézanne exhibition of seven oil paintings and thirty water colors at the Montross Gallery in January 1916. The Knoedler Gallery held no Cézanne exhibition at this period, their "Contemporary French Artists" of January 1916 being an exhibition of late impressionists.) A number of times in his work he mentions *The Blind Man*, the magazine put out for two issues by Walter Arensberg, Marcel Duchamp, and Mina Loy as propaganda for the 1917 Independents Exhibition. He refers to the affair of Duchamp's rejected urinal in his "Prologue" to *Kora in Hell: Improvisations*. He is aware of the little magazines *The Soil*, *The Seven Arts*, and *The Little Review*, Walter Arensberg's salon for painters and writers, the 1916 Forum Exhibition, and Marsden Hartley's important 1913–15 Berlin pictures.

Williams is often thought associated with Alfred Stieglitz and the Stieglitz group of painters at this time. But any real closeness to Stieglitz before the 1920s seems unlikely. Williams probably did not meet John Marin—always close to Stieglitz—or become aware that the painter was also from Rutherford, until 1922.

Williams certainly would have received little encouragement to pay close attention to the Stieglitz group from Pound. Stieglitz wrote to Pound on 3 November 1915, "Mr. Kreymborg has requested me to send you a set of '291'. A set is going to you under separate cover as well as a few copies of Camera Work." Stieglitz expressed the hope that Pound would be interested and might care to write on the subject.[1] Evidently Pound was not impressed, for writing to John Quinn in 1916 he compared the "profundity" of Wyndham Lewis to "all this modern froth—that's what it is, froth, 291, Picabia, etc., etc., etc."[2] Huntley Carter praised Stieglitz and 291 in the pages of *The Egoist,* but Carter was one of the figures Pound would have liked to remove from the magazine. Corresponding briefly with Stieglitz in 1934, Pound made it clear that he did not regard the photographer's activities as having any important implications for literature: "Naturally I have heard of you from Picabia [probably in Pound's 1920s Paris years] and in other ways for the past 20 years. But I don't know whether you regarded yr [*sic*] torchbearing as anti-literary or merely a-literary."[3]

Recalling *Al Que Quiere!* in his autobiography, Williams remembered, "Alfred Kreymborg noticed that the cacophony was a re-echoing of his name and felt complimented. We were very close friends then and I think his surmise was a proper one" (*Auto,* 157). Pound exhorted both men to get in touch with each other in the winter of 1913. Kreymborg needed material for *The Glebe*, a little magazine he was publishing at the time, and Williams was looking for a publisher. Pound had become aware of Kreymborg through John Cournos, one-time art critic of *The Philadelphia Record,* who had solicited Pound for *Glebe* material in London. (Pound sent the compilation eventually published as *Des Imagistes.*)[4]

Kreymborg was a central figure in the "Others" group of painters and writers based in Grantwood, New Jersey, and he had many connections among the avant-garde in New York. He was early acquainted with Alanson Hartpence, who from 1914 managed the Daniel Gallery, one of the few outlets for modernist artists. His autobiographical *Troubador* describes evenings spent at Kiel's Bakery in New York, around 1910, where fellow diners included Hartpence and Marsden Hartley. Hartley—shown at 291 as early as 1909—introduced Kreymborg to the Stieglitz circle. In this company, Kreymborg records, he "gradually learned that the lines of painting and sculpture complemented the lines of music and poetry; that, without drawing needless parallels, one could readily trace a relationship proving that many artists of the age, no matter what their medium, were seeking similar fundamentals and evolving individual forms." With this new awareness, he "revised his ideas considerably" thanks to "periodic visits to art galleries."[5]

Kreymborg always remained close to the Stieglitz group. When the *America and Alfred Stieglitz* collection of essays was organized by Paul Rosenfeld, Waldo Frank, Harold Ruff, Lewis Mumford and Dorothy Norman in 1933, Rosenfeld wrote to Kreymborg, "We are wondering whether you would not contribute to the first part of the volume stating Stieglitz' relations, through Camera Work and other means, to the writers. You would in all ways be the person to handle that aspect of his influence most knowingly and thoroughly."[6] But Kreymborg did not contribute to the volume, and the editors found no substitute to supply such a study.

Kreymborg's knowledge of the avant-garde served as subject matter for a number of the articles he wrote for *The Morning Telegraph* through 1914 and 1915. Together with his pieces on New York chess clubs and local "characters," appeared essays on "Stieglitz and '291'," "The New Washington Square" (in two parts), Guido Bruno, Man Ray and his wife, and Gertrude Stein. The relative positions of American writers and artists were acknowledged in the piece on the 291 gallery: "If there were just one Stieglitz, say in the literary field, American literature would see a revolution similar to that American art is enjoying. No one claims that present-day American art, as such, is as yet a definite proposition, but it is further along than American literature or music."[7]

Other American writers were also looking to the painters for new strategies. Sounding "The New Note" in the first number of *The Little Review,* Sherwood Anderson saw it symbolized by the Armory Show (which he saw in Chicago), with its "seething mass of new forms and new effects scrawled upon the canvases by the living young cubists and futurists."[8] Ibn Gabriol, reviewing Gertrude Stein's *Tender Buttons* in the same magazine, quoted Kandinsky on the repetition of words and argued that both Stein and Kandinsky were trying "to discard conventional structure, to eliminate understandable figures and forms, and to create a 'spiritual harmony.'"[9] The painters wrote—Demuth contributed a play to *The Glebe* and a poem to *The Blind Man*; Hartley and Marin wrote verse—and Kreymborg discussed Man Ray as both poet and painter in his *Morning Telegraph* article (the little magazine *Others* published Ray's poem "Three Dimensions"). Meanwhile, "Others" poet Mina Loy exhibited *Making Lampshades* at the Independents Exhibition, and William Saphier titled the December 1917 issue of *Others* "A Number for the Mind's Eye Not to Be Read Aloud." The little magazines carried art reproductions when finances permitted. Kreymborg's editorial efforts for the 1913 *Musical Advance* included setting up an art department run by Hartpence. But *Others,* always short of money, could only carry reproductions towards the end of its life, in January 1919.

The Forum Exhibition of Modern American Painters that Williams mentions in his *Egoist* letter was held at the Anderson Galleries, March 13–25, 1916. Besides an "explanatory note" by sixteen of the seventeen exhibiting painters, the catalog contained various forewords by members of the Committee and an introduction by Willard Huntington Wright, "What is Modern Painting?" Wright was singled out by Marsden Hartley in a 1917 letter to Stieglitz as one of the only two critics "with a real sense of criticism" (the other being Leo Stein).[10] While editor of the *Smart Set,* Wright had shown himself sympathetic to modern poetry by publishing Pound. In his *Forum* essay his view of the modern movements is conditioned by his advocacy of the synchromists, who saw the future direction of painting as the exploration of color effects; but his general remarks provide a useful summary of the modernist position as voiced in New York.

The modern search, Wright argues, has been "that of mastering the problem of aesthetic organization and of circumscribing the one means for obtaining ultimate and indestructible results." The "truths of modern art are no different from those of ancient art," for "modern art is the logical and natural outgrowth of ancient art; it is the art of yesterday heightened and intensified as the result of systematic and painstaking experimentation in the media of expression."[11]

Primitive art, with its lack of realistic intent, was often invoked to support the concerns of modern artists, hence Marius De Zayas's 1916 *African Negro Art: Its Influence on Modern Art.* But various writers brought the argument out in various ways. In *Cubists and Post-Impressionism,* for example, A. J. Eddy linked Cubist explorations of the human figure to studies by Dürer "published in 1528."[12] Meanwhile, the art galleries exhibited children's art and "primitive" sculpture alongside the latest modernist works. Writing of R. J. Coady's Washington Square Gallery in 1914, Kreymborg reported, "Here you find the very latest men of art from Paris side by side with the very oldest art of the past." One might come across "a number of blunt, queer faced, queer bodied, black figured representatives of that magnificently simple art—if art is the term you would lower it to—Congo sculpture. One is almost tempted to cry: 'Why, here are the fathers of Gauguin and Matisse and Picasso.'"[13] Robert Coady's little magazine *The Soil* published photographs of Pompeian frescoes and of primitive art, along with work by Picasso and Gris. *Camera Work* carried a Stieglitz photograph of the November 1914 Negro Art Exhibition at 291.

These ideas were incorporated into the art itself in various ways. John Marin, for example, retained a sense of the oriental forebears behind his frenetic watercolors. A number of artists used the subject of dance to express the primitive impulse behind their modern exploration of form. Man Ray's *Invention-Dance* was one of his *Forum* pictures, and Demuth's satanic *The Dancer* (1917) was shown at the Independents Exhibition.

Many painterly allusions in Williams's work at this time are linked to elemental forces. The poet/painter is often represented as a rising sun—new expression born out of a timeless cycle. And creative unity is presented as the resolution of highly charged sexual tensions. In "Tract" (1916), the "townspeople" can better "a troop / of artists" by matching the funeral they are to "perform" with the primitive and dignified nature of death itself. In the same issue of *Others* in which "Tract" appeared, Kreymborg wrote a reply. Williams's own coffin is to reflect these "primitive" and visual arts interests.

> To W.C.W.M.D.
>
> . . . On yours
> yellow and orange nasturtium
> with a grain of red earth!
> And a design, sir,
> six lanky grasshoppers
> with knees and toes a-jump—
> W.C.W.M.D.
> on yours let's have a design![14]

In a similar "primitive" vein, *Poetry* published children's verse, the spontaneity of the young versifiers supposedly being uncontaminated by outmoded, repressive rules of art. In the *Al Que Quiere!* poems children sometimes figure as the source of the artistic values being sought. One example is "The murderer's little daughter" of "Sympathetic Portrait of a Child" (1916), with "the knife / that darts along her smile." Another is "K. McB" (1916), who can subsume her identity into the "dignity" of the earth.

Huntington Wright made another important point in his *Forum* catalog discussion. "The impelling dictate of all great art," he argued, has been "the search for composition." "The objects, whether arbitrary or photographic, which an artist uses in a picture are only the material through which plastic form finds expression." Therefore, he concludes, "If in the works of truly significant art there is a dramatic, narrative or illustrative interest, it will be found to be the incidental and not the important concomitant of the picture." With the coming of modern art, the illustrative aspect of painting had tended "toward minimization." For Wright, the logical outcome of this process was the pure color explorations of synchronism, but his advice on how to look at a modern painting applied to all the modern schools: "To judge a picture competently, one must not consider it as a mere depiction of life or as an anecdote: one must bring to it an intelligence capable of grasping a complicated counterpoint."[15]

Williams was learning to build a "complicated counterpoint" into his work as he moved towards the improvisations of *Kora in Hell* and the complex patterning of the poems and prose in *Spring and All*. Indicative of his growing ability to allow juxtaposition and contrast, instead of narrative, to establish structure are the changes he made in "Lyric" (1915) when it became "Chickory and Daisies" (*CEP,* 122) in *Al Que Quiere!.* "Lyric" first appeared in *Rogue,* the short-lived little magazine put out by Arensberg's friends Allen and Louise Norton.

> Lift your flowers
> On bitter stems
> Chickory!
> Lift them up
> Out of the scorched ground!
> Bear no foliage
> But give yourself
> Wholly to that!
> Strain under them
> You bitter stems
> That no beast eats—
> And scorn greyness!
> Into the heat with them:
> Cool,
> Luxuriant,
> Sky blue!
> The earth cracks and shrivels up
> The wind moans piteously
> The sky goes out
> If you should fail.
>   Reflect.
> I saw a child with daisies
> For weaving into the hair
> Tear the stems
> With her teeth.[16]

Each line begins with a capital. The poem is made narrative by the poet's resolution to "Reflect" upon its two parts, the word itself providing the pivot from one stanza to the other. The poet must "Reflect" upon the apostrophe to the flower, and upon his observation of a child committing the destruction that is a necessary prelude to composition. In *Al Que Quiere!* the two sections stand separated, numbered I and II, and "Reflect" is omitted. No longer is the *poet* to "reflect," now it is the reader who must "bring to it an intelligence capable of grasping a complicated counterpoint." The new title, "Chickory and Daisies," offers a more interesting presentation of these lines as a new kind of poem than does "Lyric," raising questions of the composition's relationship to the two separate perceptions that the title and the "counterpoint" unite, but which the poet in his poem has deliberately sundered. In his greater confidence,

Williams dispenses with some capitals, allowing the poem the freedom to impose its own rhythm upon grammar.

The next important show following the Forum Exhibition was the First Independents Exhibition, held from 10 April to 6 May 1917. In conjunction with the event, Henri Pierre Roche published a magazine, *The Blind Man,* for two issues from Walter Arensberg's address. Contributors included Mina Loy, Arensberg, Marcel Duchamp, Robert Carlton Brown and Demuth. The first issue of 10 April invoked Whitman in a paean to the iconoclastic spirit.

> May the spirit of Walt Whitman guide the Indeps
> Long live his memory and long live the Indeps![17]

The final issue the following month led off with the "Richard Mutt" affair. Duchamp, in accordance with his theory of "ready-mades" and to test the open policy of the exhibition—any artist paying the $6 fee could exhibit—had submitted a signed urinal. "Mr. Mutt's fountain" was refused by the jury, and *The Blind Man* took up the accusation that the object was vulgar and not "art." It was not immoral, the magazine argued, but a fixture seen every day in plumbers' windows. And as for "art," it was irrelevant that the object was not made by the artist for "He CHOSE it. He took an ordinary article of life, placed it so that its useful significance disappeared under the new title and point of view—created a new thought for that object."[18] In 1917, Williams was inclined to be critical (although the following year—in the "Prologue" to *Kora in Hell: Improvisations*—he recognized the importance of the issues raised). In a 1917 review of the little magazines he wrote, "Such things as *The Blind Man* are very useful, very 'purgative,' very nice decoration, even very true." But he thought it "rather naive" and felt that "chaos is somewhat overdone." His opinion of Demuth's poem "For Richard Mutt" was his opinion of the whole affair: "but—ici il n'y a pas grand chose."[19]

Williams's comments in the review on R. J. Coady's magazine *The Soil* are similar. It too is merely "decorative." He found its poetry (much of it by the "Literary Editor" Enrique Cross) "trivial," and though he liked the magazine's energy, he was not impressed by its "apotheosis of trust magnates and trip hammers and Jack Johnsons."[20] But along with photographs of boxers and locomotives, Coady published reproductions of modernist and primitive art from his Washington Square Gallery exhibitions. He took an independent, aggressively nationalistic stance towards what was required of indigenous art. Though he admired some of the French painters, he was critical of American artists who slavishly copied the latest fashions from Paris. In the pages of *The Soil* he jibed at the Independents Exhibition, "To exhibit a large number of paintings and sculptures, the best of which were foreign, and the rest of which were a la foreign, shows neither an adjustment to local life nor a broad and liberal independence for which the Society has blown its horn."[21] He took out space in the Forum Exhibition catalog to ask of the paintings, "Why are they American, what element or elements, quality or qualities, do they possess that make them American?" Coady's ideas of an American art based upon American technology and popular culture were ahead of their time in many ways. When he died in 1921, he was the subject of a warm tribute by his friend Robert Alden Sanborn in the magazine *Broom.*

Williams moved closer to Coady's ideas when he edited his own magazine *Contact* in the early twenties. Coady was an enthusiastic admirer of the painter Juan Gris, whose synthetic cubism became so important for Williams in *Spring and All.* Williams's 1921 essay "A Matisse" echoes Coady's warnings on the slavish imitation of French artists, while the products of American popular culture are an important theme in some of the *Spring and All* poems. Erroneously, but tellingly, in his autobiography he remembers *The Soil* as "later" than *The Seven Arts* (*Auto,* 197).

Williams thought *The Seven Arts* "a brave pioneer in discretion . . . made for middle-aged, semi-brave revolutionists who have fixed their canons of taste beyond question."[22] He also thought *The Masses* too indulgent of the comfort of its audience, while his early supporter, *Poetry*—no longer associated with Pound—was "amiable," a kind way to lament Harriet Monroe's lack of editorial discrimination.[23]

Of all the modernist painters, it is the work of Marsden Hartley at this time that provides the most useful parallel to developments in Williams's thinking. Both poet and painter had a strong interest in Kandinsky's work. Either Demuth or Kreymborg could have turned Williams's attention to Hartley. Hartley met Demuth in Paris in 1912 and introduced him to Stieglitz in 1914. The two painters became close friends in the fall and winter of 1916, working together at Provincetown and later in Bermuda.

Kreymborg's acquaintance with Hartley dated back to the evenings at Kiel's Bakery, and the two kept up a correspondence that lasted into the 1930s, when Hartley still gave Kreymborg news of Williams as of an old mutual friend. Kreymborg certainly saw Hartley's first Berlin pictures at 291 in January 1914. His account to *Morning Telegraph* readers later that year of what they might expect from a first visit to 291 included a description of Hartley's Berlin work. "Don't let the place scare you," he advised. "You may see a lot of flying triangles on the walls or some yellow epaulettes and weird trumpets and green rhomboids. Some one may tell you you are looking at Marsden Hartley."[24]

Hartley was regularly shown at 291 after 1909. In the spring of 1912 he traveled to Paris, then later moved to Berlin. In Munich he met Kandinsky and Marc, and wrote to Stieglitz in praise of their paintings and theoretical work. Apart from a brief visit to New York in connection with his 1914 exhibition, he did not return to the United States until December 1915, when he was forced back by the collapse of the German art market. Hartley's work passed through a number of styles before his 1913–15 Berlin pictures, but these were the canvases that Williams first remembered, and most admired, when writing of him in later years.

Hartley was the only important American modernist painter exposed at first hand to the work of the German expressionists, although Demuth probably visited him briefly in Berlin. The European section of the Armory Show was almost entirely French, with a sole Kandinsky, *Improvisation No. 27,* representing important European developments outside France. Stieglitz purchased the painting, and subsequently wrote to Kandinsky expressing interest in his work and sounding out the possibilities for an exhibition at 291. But the exhibition did not materialize.

Hartley was impressed with Kandinsky's *Ueber das Geistige in der Kunst,* which struck a chord with his own strain of mysticism. Nevertheless, as a staunch advocate of art as the personal expression of its creator, he soon sought to distance himself from Kandinsky by asserting that his own personality was distinctly American. Regretting that some modern art had become coldly impersonal, he asked in his note to the Forum Exhibition catalog, "I am wondering why the autographic is so negligible, why the individual has ceased to register himself. . . . That which is expressed in a drawing or painting is certain to tell who is its creator."[25] (In accordance with his belief, Hartley rarely signed or dated his canvases, a circumstance that has caused problems for students of his work.)

Between his 1912–13 Kandinsky-style "Movements" and his Berlin pictures of 1913–15, Hartley aimed at a personal form of expression that would capture the pageantry, color, and emotion of the sights he perceived around him. While stressing the individuality of his response, he wished to convey the elemental nature both of the sights and of his interaction with them. The resulting style utilized vibrant primary colors, solid geometrical construction, sometimes of recognizable objects, and a looseness of formal relationship sufficient to suggest the spontaneity of the emotional encounter. Hartley felt that his art had moved away from symbolism to a style that allowed his creative response to the world to be sufficient justification for the structure of his compositions. In a foreword to his 1914 exhibition he argued, "It is the artist's business to select forms suitable to his own specialized experience, forms which express naturally the emotions he personally desires to present, leaving conjectures and discussions to take care of themselves.'' ''The idea of modernity,'' he went on, ''is but a new attachment to things universal—a fresh relationship to the courses of the sun and to the living swing of the earth. . . . The new wonder of the moment.''[26] Examples of ''things universal'' that frequently appear in these pictures are the sun, the cross, the triangle, and the communal chalice and wafer. In the 1912 *Handsome Drinks,* the chalice and wafer are ranged alongside more secular refreshments from Parisian bars. Immediately to the left of the chalice, the letters L U S allow the vessel itself to suggest the concluding T. These religious objects are also part of the ''things universal'' that make up *Painting No. 48* (1913), where a figure ''8'' is stamped upon the central, dominating wafer-shape, and in the left corner a flaming sun encloses a cross.

In *Camera Work* Charles Caffin reviewed this 1914 exhibition sympathetically. He characterized the emotional power behind the canvases as ''neither of intellectual nor spiritual experience,'' rather it was of ''sensuous emotion.'' ''The whole is a strangely interesting exposure of the throes of a soul in labor, and leaves me wondering what will be the result of parturition.''[27]

A number of 1914 drawings are called simply *Symbols*. The 1914 oil *Indian Symbols* turns Kandinsky's triangle into a series of Indian wigwams and seated chiefs in headdress. But works such as *Composition* (1914) and *Berlin Ante-War* (1915) are looser in construction. More varied shapes interact upon the canvas, with ambiguous sexual forms expressing part of the operative tension. By the time of his April 1916 exhibition Hartley stressed less the ''forms'' that expressed his experience than the visual experience itself: ''There is no hidden symbolism whatsoever in them; there is no slight intention of that anywhere. . . . They are merely consultations of the eye—in no sense problem; my notion of the purely pictural.''[28] Again impressed, Charles Caffin explained Hartley's fusion of ''the intangibility of abstract expression'' with details that were ''recognizably concrete'' in terms of the difference between the rejected ''hidden symbolism'' and the use of objects as ''symbols of expression.''[29]

In November 1916 *The Little Review* published an account by Charlotte Teller of a visit to Hartley in his Berlin studio. In Hartley's room, ''colors refuse to fade, but stay sharp and clean like good morals.'' Hartley's fidelity to the demands of the canvas allowed him to produce work whose significance bursts beyond physical and temporal confines: ''The motion set up by color and line goes sweeping out beyond the frame, beyond the walls of the room, beyond Berlin and Europe and the age we live in. . . .'' In describing one of the canvases, the writer brought out the sexual element: "It expresses his feeling of what he calls 'ecstasy' on the part of the dragoons at the manoevers he had seen. A rising dome, the eternal symbol of endeavor weighted by the desires of the flesh. . . . And in this dome, and on either side, white horses, mounting, red trappings, white uniforms, and black boots; all of them pointing upward to a high point somewhere far outside the painting itself."[30]

Teller's description could well be of *The Warriors* (1914), unsold at the time of Hartley's death. However, the general tenor of her remarks could equally apply to many of the Berlin works. *Berlin Ante-War* (1914), for example, is dominated by a sunlike, yellow circle in its top half, the circle set against solid white cloud forms lined with yellow. From below, the circle is penetrated by the body of a figure on horseback. The lower canvas contains a stylized pudendum pattern, its lines rippling outwards towards the edges of its prescribed space. Within the pattern's curves lies another sun and the blue and white squares of what could be a chess board. One of the four squared-off scenes to right and left of this pattern is a rising (or setting) sun.

In Hartley's Berlin work the personal, the immediate, and the "things universal" blend into a vibrant pattern. Matching such fusion in his verse, Williams could move away from merely stating his excitement, as he had in the uncollected "At Dawn" (1914): "O Marvellous! what new configuration will come next? / I am bewildered with multiplicity."[31] Confident now of the structural validity of the composition produced by his emotional engagement, instead of passively watching the mythology-soaked heavens of the earlier poem as they choreograph their "war of the skies," he can face "the hollow vastness of the sky" of "Dawn," (1917). This poem both describes its own creation, and presents the created pattern, in painterly terms.

> Ecstatic bird songs pound
> the hollow vastness of the sky
> with metallic clinkings—
> beating color up into it
> at a far edge,—beating it, beating it
> with rising, triumphant ardor,—
> stirring it into warmth,
> quickening in it a spreading change,—
> bursting wildly against it as
> dividing the horizon, a heavy sun
> lifts himself—is lifted—
> bit by bit above the edge
> of things,—runs free at last
> out into the open—! lumbering
> glorified in full release upward—
> songs cease.
>
> (*CEP,* 138)

His "songs" are the poet/painter's tools as he hammers out his work (in *Al Que Quiere!* three poems are titled "Love Song" and one "Summer Song"). "Songs cease" with successful composition. The poet's materials take on his "ardor" as he works with them and achieves mastery over them. The poem is rooted in personal expression, insisting that its materials and structure gain their significance, not from conventions of representation, but by the poet's manipulation of them in his creative ecstasy. The method and purpose are similar to those of Hartley's Berlin pictures. The kind of painting alluded to in "Dawn" has more in common with those colorful, expressive works than with the muted color in the formal explorations of cubism. The similarity of sexual imagery in the Williams and the Berlin works makes the parallel even closer. It is part of the "spreading change" of "Dawn" that its hammered colors and shapes take on a sexual purport as "dividing the horizon, a heavy sun / lifts himself—is lifted." The surprise of the sun dividing the horizon rather than the reverse image emphasizes the allusion to sexual penetration.

"Virtue" (1917) is another correlation of sex, creativity, and painting. The first stanza presents sexual invitation in terms of color shapes moving upon each other.

> Now? Why—
> whirlpools of
> orange and purple flame
> feather twists of chrome
> on a green ground
> funneling down upon
> the steaming phallus-head
> of the mad sun himself—
> blackened crimson!

The act of accepting such an invitation becomes

> nothing—
> but the fixing of an eye
> concretely upon emptiness!

The "Virtue" of the title lies in the courage of the sexual/artistic embrace with "the vulgar inviting mouth of her." Preconceived relationships of marriage, of poetic form, and of pictorial pattern to conventional representations of nature are irrelevant to the demand of the "Now . . . Come!" While still encumbered by such preconceptions, the artist lacks the "emptiness''—the mental and artistic freedom—upon which to build his composition solely on its own terms, and his. The encounter is akin to that undertaken by "the painters following Cézanne," who, according to Williams in his autobiography, had the courage to view pictorial composition as "sheer paint: a picture a matter of pigments upon a piece of cloth stretched on a frame" (*Auto*, 380).

The poem also incorporates Williams's sexual theories, discussed in the previous chapter. Taking *The Egoist*'s Dora Marsden to task for what he considered her confusion of "male and female psychology," he argued that the subject was an important one because her view represented a "covert attack on the 'creative artist.'"[32] In a subsequent letter he set out his own distinction. Part of this was that outside of the pursuit of the female and the sex function, "man has absolutely no necessity to exist."[33] Thus we find the cluster of males ranged alongside the one inviting female in the poem.

> Come! here are—
> cross-eyed men, a boy
> with a patch, men walking
> in their shirts, men in hats
> dark men, a pale man
> with little black moustaches
> and a dirty white coat,
> fat men with pudgy faces,
> thin faces, crooked faces
> slit eyes, grey eyes, black eyes
> old men with dirty beards,
> men in vests with
> gold watch chains. Come!
>   (*CEP*, 152–53)

But each one of the male figures listed in this last stanza represents a potential encounter as fertile as the rich colors and movement of the opening lines.

The male-female pursuit is suggested with greater economy in "Spring Strains" (1916) as two birds chase a third.

> two blue-grey birds chasing
> a third struggle in circles, angles,
> swift convergings to a point that bursts
>   instantly!
>   . . . the blinding and red-edged sun-blur—
> creeping energy, concentrated
> counterforce—welds sky, buds, trees,
> rivets them in one puckering hold!

> Sticks through! Pulls the whole
> counter-pulling mass upward, to the right
> locks even the opaque, not yet defined
> ground in a terrific drag that is
> loosening the very tap-roots!
>
> On a tissue-thin monotone of blue-grey buds
> two blue-grey birds, chasing a third,
> at full cry! Now they are
> flung outward and up—disappearing suddenly!
>
> (*CEP,* 159)

Motion is imparted to the spinning circle by its male elements. The sexual union at "Sticks through!" removes the birds from being "in" to being "on" the composition born of the encounter. The shift in preposition underscores the painterly aspect of the achieved pattern.

It must have been the common interests of sexual theorizing and early painterly aspirations, together with their sharing mixed racial origins that led Williams in "Foreign" (1917) to compare himself with the Russian writer Mikhail Artsybashev. (The poem appeared in *Al Que Quiere!* but Williams did not reprint it.) The author of *Sanine* was in vogue at the time, the Chicago *Dial* noting in September 1915 "the third volume of M. Artzibashef's to be published in English translation within less than a year."[34] (*Rogue* published some of his work in December 1916.) *Sanine* has been characterized as an "apologia for unrestrained sexual expression and revolt against all authority," and Artsybashev's view of life as "a procession of human bodies filled with animal desire and slowly moving to the grave."[35] A fan wrote to *The Dial* pointing out that Artsybashev was "an admixture of five races." "He has told of his grief," the writer went on, "at not being able to devote his life to painting upon canvas; but he possesses the great gift of handling words as colors, and his books are worth reading for this alone."[36] Williams's poem is little more than a loose musing upon possible parallels in the daily lives of the two men, but the association is an interesting indication of his interests in 1917.

Compositional patterning based upon sexual tension is what is finally demanded in "To a Solitary Disciple" (1916). Again, it is dawn. The interlocking forms of the scene rather than its incidental colors are to be noticed.

> Rather notice, mon cher,
> that the moon is
> tilted above
> the point of the steeple
> than that its color
> is shell-pink.

Rather observe
that it is early morning
than that the sky
is smooth
as a turquoise.

Rather grasp
how the dark
converging lines
of the steeple
meet at the pinnacle—
perceive how
its little ornament
tries to stop them—

This poem appeared in *Others* in a group that included "Metric Figure" ("Veils of clarity / have succeeded / veils of color"), and that poem could be a general commentary upon the specific lesson in perception offered here. The lines of the steeple force themselves past decoration. Protective of "the flower," they also extend to protect "the eaten moon." The compositional patterning reduces the perceived objects to their geometric elements, to "the point," "the hexagonal spire," and "the converging lines." The final presentation of the contending sexual forces conveys both resolution and contention.

It is true:
in the light colors
of morning
brown-stone and slate
shine orange and dark blue.

But observe
the oppressive weight
of the squat edifice!
Observe
the jasmine lightness
of the moon.
                    (*CEP,* 167–68)

Williams's commentators have often associated this poem with Demuth's "ray-line" paintings of steeples, but these paintings follow the painter's late 1916 interest in Cézanne and analytical cubism. Williams has probably used the view from his own front door at 9 Ridge Road. Rutherford's First Presbyterian Church differs from the church of "To a Solitary Disciple" only in having an octagonal instead of a hexagonal spire. But the church is built of brown stone and the spire is slate, while the sprawl of the building in relation to its short spire certainly makes "squat" an appropriate description.

Perhaps Williams deliberately changed the number of facets upon the spire to distance the composition from his doorstep perception. A similar kind of shift is neatly produced in "Summer Song" (1916) as the poet addresses the "wanderer moon."

> if I should
> buy a shirt
> your color and
> put on a necktie
> sky-blue
> where would they carry me?
> (*CEP,* 135)

The shift from "your" to "they" emphasizes the separation of the ar-ranged composition from the object in nature supplying the initial impe-tus. From such separation, the poem achieves its own successful "lift." This is again a sexual union, for the necktie is associated with the female muse of "The Wanderer"—Williams's grandmother. In that poem, the poet dresses for his journey to the Passaic: "In my woolen shirt and the pale-blue necktie   /   My grandmother gave me, there I went" (*CEP,* 11).

Perhaps it was "Summer Song" that William Saphier had in mind when the Chicago-based art critic, painter, and "Others" poet published an "Improvisation of William Carlos Williams" in the May 1917 *Little Review.* Upon a round sun or moon face, the simple geometry of the facial features includes "breasts" for cheeks, an acute-angled triangle for a nose, with thin slits of eyebrows suggestive of just concluded sleep and the imminent rising of the pupils over the horizon of the brows. The whole face sails light and serene across the open spaces of the white behind it.[37]

The general compositional strategy behind many of the poems of *Al Que Quiere!,* and the use they make of painterly elements, inform Wil-liams's praise of his friend Maxwell Bodenheim in "MB" (1917).

> Winter has spent this snow
> out of envy, but spring is here!
> He sits at the breakfast table
> in his yellow hair
> and disdains even the sun
> walking outside
> in spangled slippers:
>
> He looks out: there is
> a glare of lights
> before a theater,—

a sparkling lady
passes quickly to
the seclusion of
her carriage.

Presently
under the dirty, wavy heaven
of a borrowed room he will make
reinhaled tobacco smoke
his clouds and try them
against the sky's limits!

(*CEP,* 144)

Sitting down to write, "MB" with his yellow hair produces his own light, "and disdains even the sun." Looking out at artistic arrangement of light, and tuning into feminine expression, he prepares to compose. But the composition is within his own terms—the room borrowed for the nonce— as he strives to become the sun within the clouds of his own tobacco smoke. "MB" moves from notice of external nature ("this snow") to perceived artistic relationship that bears an oblique relationship to the gestation occuring within the poet ("a glare of lights / before a theater") and finally to re-expression of this arrangement in personal terms with forms of the artist's own choosing.

Before publication of *Al Que Quiere!* Williams had entertained the notion of subtitling the book "The Pleasures of Democracy." The November 1915 *Others* carried the comment by J. B. Kerfoot on the magazine that, "It is the expression of a democracy of feeling rebelling against an aristocracy of form." The sentence sums up Williams's intention. The volume was to be American expression rebelling against the conventions of European form, and contemporary expression rebelling against conventions suited to past eras. But the Spanish title, which means "To Him Who Wants It," emphasizes that the poems are suitable only for a limited readership. As Pound and many others had stressed, modernist art was essentially "undemocratic" in its refusal to compromise to gain an audience. Perhaps thinking of Pound's new Chinese interests, in a letter to Marianne Moore, Williams likened the "not democratic" Spanish title to "a Chinese image cut out of stone," and admitted that it "does not truly represent the contents of the book" (*SL*, 40). Instead of using the subtitle, his solution was to design a cover based upon another kind of "image" from a stone. He remembered in *I Wanted to Write a Poem*: "The figure on the cover was taken from a design on a pebble. To me the design looked like a dancer, and the effect of the dancer was very important— a natural, completely individual pattern. The artist made the outline around the design too geometrical; it should have been irregular, as the pebble was" (*IWWP*, 18).

The balance Williams tried to focus by giving the book two titles is the balance he sought between organization that was more than idiosyncratic yet rooted in the creative patterning of his own experience, and not in pre-existing conventions. The achievement of this balance is the theme of many of the *Al Que Quiere!* poems and accounts for their central concern with the process of composition.

In August 1917 Pound declared, "Any work of art is a compound of freedom and order. It is perfectly obvious that art hangs between chaos on one side and mechanics on the other."[38] But by the end of 1917 Williams and Kreymborg both had doubts about Pound's particular resolution. In December's *The Little Review* Kreymborg found him too tied to tradition.

> no man can essay a pavanne
> with his phrases at variance—
> it *is* a pavanne, don't deny it!
> And why propose a pavanne
> when nobody dances pavannes . . .
> Dear dunce
> your tune begins to sound feminine[39]

For Williams, Pound, together with "Fletcher and Eliot and Stevens," was "going over the forms of yesterday and making fine stuff to read and enjoy." Williams demanded, instead of such repetition, a rigorous rethinking of the structure of verse to match the painters' redefinition at the level of line. "The elements of the new form must be simple and single so that they are capable of every form of moulding."[40] However, few of Williams's *Al Que Quiere!* poems give the sense of being molded from such "simple and single" units. They exhibit only a limited breaking of syntax and play with the expected word—strategies important in the poetry to come. And if one kind of narrative has been undercut, presenting the narrative of compositional strategy in poem after poem builds up its own set of conventions. "Simple and single" is more applicable to the disjunctions wrought in Williams's prose improvisations in *Kora in Hell*, which in the fall of 1917 were beginning to appear in *The Little Review*, than to the poems of *Al Que Quiere!*. If art hung between "chaos" and "mechanics," Williams was preparing to take a closer look at the "chaos" he had found "overdone" when reviewing *The Blind Man*, to integrate the iconoclasm of Duchamp with the expressionism of Kandinsky. In *Kora in Hell: Improvisations* he would "let the imagination have its own way to see if it could save itself" (*Imag*, 116).

4

Kora in Hell: Improvisations

With his next book, *Kora in Hell: Improvisations,* Williams explicitly allied his demand for new form with the work of the painters, and set
himself against many of the contemporary trends in verse that he saw
around him. As far as Williams was concerned, Pound, his new discovery
T. S. Eliot, and also such poets as Edgar Lee Masters, Robert Frost, and
Vachel Lindsay, were merely repeating the old forms. It was the painters
that were taking the bold new directions. In the "Prologue" to the improvisations he declares, "If the inventive imagination must look, as I
think, to the field of art for its richest discoveries today it will best make
its way by compass and follow no path (*Imag,* 13–14)."

The painters were brave enough to "invent," rather than merely take
comfort in established structures; Williams presents his improvisations as
such an exercise in the "inventive imagination." In *Kora in Hell,* Williams
breaks up many of the calculated effects of language—alliteration, meter,
repetition—that remained the stuff even of the new *vers libre.* He takes
as his rationale Kandinsky's notion of an "improvisation," and Duchamp's theory of "ready-mades," and establishes his affinity with the
visual artists by peppering the "Prologue" and the improvisations with
the names of painters: Gleizes, Man Ray, Demuth, Duchamp, the painter
of "cigar-box-cover-like nudes," Kandinsky, "a little English-woman,
A.E. Kerr," Cézanne, Rackham, Rembrandt, Titian, Dürer, Teniers
Velázquez, and Botticelli.

Kora in Hell: Improvisations was published on 1 September 1920.
Approximately three-quarters of the improvisations in the first half of the
book had been published in *The Little Review* in October 1917, January
1918, and June 1919, but without their accompanying italicized "commentaries." The "Prologue," which Williams dated 1 September 1918,
appeared in the same magazine in two parts, in April and May 1919.

In his autobiography Williams describes how *Kora in Hell* came to
be written.

I decided that I would write something every day, without missing one day, for a year. I'd write nothing planned but take up a pencil, put the paper before me, and write anything that came into my head. . . . I did just that, day after day, without missing one day for a year. Not a word was to be changed. I didn't change any, but I did tear up some of the stuff. (*Auto,* 158)

The "Prologue" and the improvisations that were published in *The Little Review* do appear in the book in substantially the same form—even the same order—as in the journal. But Williams had some overall pattern in view, for he wrote to his publisher Edmund Brown on 27 January 1919 that he was "not through with my arrangement and other detail."[1]

As frontispiece to the volume Williams chose a drawing by the American painter Stuart Davis, and later explained his reasons: "It was, graphically, exactly what I was trying to do with words, put the Improvisations down as a unit on the page . . . an impressionistic view of the simultaneous (*IWWP,* 29)." This frontispiece presents a montage of various scenes of Gloucester, Massachusetts. The drawing, similar to a number that Davis executed between 1915 and 1919, emphasizes the artist's determination to abandon the conventions of perspective that would dictate the size and positioning of his scenes, and instead to explore other kinds of formal relationship.

Davis had begun his career as a disciple of the ashcan school, and his subject matter in the drawing remains that of urban life. After the Armory Show he moved towards a modern idiom that eventually, in the twenties and thirties, became almost completely abstract. But in this drawing his style follows the manipulation of perspective, introduced by Cézanne, through breaking up solid objects into a number of parts. Cézanne had stretched the possibilities of painting by simplifying representational figures according to the demands of his own formal concept, and by rejecting the unities demanded by traditional techniques of perspective. An apple or plate on a table, for example, is painted with an attention to local detail that ignores the limitations that the painting's apparent angle of vision would impose. The conventions of representing temporal and spatial relationships are transcended as the painting imposes its own order. When the analytical cubists extended Cézanne's innovations, dissecting such motifs as a violin or an absinthe bottle in their paintings, they patterned their canvases with multiple views of the object that could not be seen from a single perspective. Davis did not dissect individual objects in his 1916–18 work, but he broke up perspective and ignored conventional relationships of compositional form. The figures, buildings, and animals of Gloucester are rearranged by the artist to his own purpose. No longer representing ideas and relationships external to the work itself, they function as units of form, of equal value in their role as expressions of the artist's intent. As one of the italicized sections of *Kora* puts it: "The perfections revealed by a Rembrandt are equal whether it be question of a laughing Saskia or an old woman cleaning her nails" (*Imag,* 41).

Williams did not know Davis personally, but he could have seen his work at the Independents Exhibition, or at the December 1917–January 1918 *Exhibition of Landscapes* at the Whitney Studio. He could also have seen Davis's first one-man show, held at the Sheridan Square Gallery, Brooklyn. He obtained Davis's address from Alanson Hartpence at the Daniel Gallery, and in forwarding it Hartpence took occasion to express scorn at Davis's lingering ashcan traits: "Stuart Davis looks blearily at the medium of painting through sociologic eyes. . . . This bleary vieu [sic] serves to blear and generally mess up his medium."[2] But a comment by Davis from 1918 shows his formal concerns as similar to those of Williams in *Kora*: "Fourteenth Century demanded plot relationship of subject, 1870–1918 demanded plastic relationship of subject, 1918—demands plastic expression of mental scope."[3] Williams must have been gratified at the painter's enthusiastic response upon receiving the published book: "I see it as a fluidity as opposed to stagnation of presentation. It opens a field of possibilities. To me it suggests a development of word against word without any impediment of story, poetic beauty or anything at all except word clash and sequence."[4]

But in the twenties, as most American modernist painters abandoned abstraction, Davis began to embrace it. Williams soon lost interest in his work, regarding it as merely a copy of the Continental style. In 1921 he lamented to Kenneth Burke: "I went to see . . . a show of pictures by Stuart Davis etc. [probably at the Whitney Studio Club] Very nice but rather disappointing. God when will an American be born?"[5]

The improvisations operate as "an impressionistic view of the simultaneous" in a number of ways. One of these is in their treatment of past art. Kandinsky's formula (which Williams quotes in the "Prologue") met with his approval because it posits personal and contemporary expression as the starting point of art, and "the pure and eternal qualities of the art of all men" as the result. Those poets, such as Pound and Eliot, whom Williams classed in the "Prologue" as "men content with the connotations of their masters" (*Imag,* 24), by inverting this process, allowed traditional forms to muffle their contemporary expression, and failed to achieve the simultaneous presentation of past and present that realized these "pure and eternal qualities."

In the *Al Que Quiere!* poems that deal with the relationship of past art to the poet's contemporary task, Williams uses the devices of juxtaposition, and of placing the whole poem in the present tense, with the result that the emphasis falls upon the challenge of the moment, not the triumphs of the past. The same devices are incorporated into *Kora in Hell*. Both the improvisations and the italicized commentaries are couched in the present tense. Thus while the commentaries appear to distance the improvisations, they do not do so in terms of time. In fact, improvisations and commentaries lock together in a dialectic that denies the possibility of a pattern based upon spatial or temporal distance, paralleling the strategy of post-Cézanne painting. There is no constant relationship between the two kinds of passage that would permit a conclusive summary (save a mathematical one, discussed below). Sometimes a commentary provides background to the immediately preceding improvisation, sometimes to the preceding two or three. Sometimes a passage of commentary bears little or no apparent relationship to what immediately precedes or comes after it, and may instead offer one interpretation of the strategy behind the improvisations as a whole. By avoiding the constant of some larger relationship, Williams calls attention to the particular—his units of form: words, sentences, and passages—and emphasizes the relationship of these particulars as primarily an aesthetic one. When the modernist painters eliminated the single viewpoint, which had accompanied the effect of depth in painting, they withdrew the gauge by which the viewer could bring his habitual set of representational expectations to bear upon the work. Similarly in *Kora in Hell,* the past exists in no time *beyond,* and tradition imposes no obligations. Past art is caught up in the process that becomes the contemporary work of art. Later, in *Spring and All* and *In the American Grain,* Williams uses a similar multidirectional technique to suggest the compression of all American experience into the single moment of contemporary pressure captured by his compositional pattern.

When Williams reviewed *The Blind Man* in his essay "America, Whitman, and the Art of Poetry" he found the magazine's concerns interesting, but of minor importance. But in his attempt to reconcile spontaneity with the patterning of form in his improvisations, he realized the parallels between the issues raised by Marcel Duchamp's theory of "ready-mades" and the direction of his own thinking. In the "Prologue" to the improvisations he declares that the affair of "the porcelain urinal . . . should not be allowed to slide into oblivion." And he offers an account of Duchamp's practice in creating a "ready-made."

> One day Duchamp decided that his composition for that day would be the first thing that struck his eye in the first hardware store he should enter. It turned out to be a pickax [actually the shovel that became *In Advance of the Broken Arm,* 1915] which he bought and set up in his studio. This was his composition. (*Imag,* 10)

Williams emphasizes the visual priority behind the creation of the ready-made. First the eye is "struck," then the application of the discovery follows. In *Spring and All* he described the method of the improvisations in similar terms, using "imagination" to describe this state of visual readiness.

> The *Improvisations* . . . I had recourse to the expedient of letting life go completely in order to live in the world of my choice.
> I let the imagination have its own way to see if it could save itself. (*Imag*, 116)

There is a similarity between Duchamp's own account of the philosophy behind ready-mades and Williams's description of the regular nocturnal routine behind the writing of the improvisations. When Duchamp decided to produce a ready-made he would prepare himself for a "rendezvous."

> The important thing then is just this matter of timing, this snapshot effect, like a speech delivered on no matter what occasion but at *such and such an hour*. It is a kind of rendez-vous.
> Naturally inscribe that date, hour, minute, on the ready-made as information.[6]

Williams gave a dateline to his "Prologue" to suggest its composition as the result of a single sitting. As with Duchamp's strategy, there is no time for rational thought to impose conventional patterns upon the composition.

Duchamp was very much in the news in the years immediately following the Armory Show. He arrived in the United States in June 1915, staying until the summer of 1918. He found a patron in Walter Arensberg—the first benefactor of *Others*—and also formed a close friendship with Charles Demuth. Williams was thus well placed for information on Duchamp's latest exploits, although his personal relationship to the Frenchman appears to have remained a distant one. (Pound suggested in 1922, "You ought to meet Marcel Duchamp. He is now in N.Y.")[7]

But whatever their personal relationship, Duchamp's work clearly interested Williams, and his autobiography, essays, "Prologue," and improvisations document this interest. In the "Prologue," he describes lunching with Arensberg and viewing the version of *A Nude Descending the Staircase* that Duchamp created for his patron by painting over a full-size photographic print of the original. (Arensberg subsequently purchased the original, which had been the sensation of the Armory Show and had been acquired by A. J. Eddy). Williams comments in the "Prologue," "by the technique of its manufacture as by other means it is a novelty" (*Imag*, 9), inviting a parallel with his own calculated arrangement of spontaneous thoughts in the improvisations. This was the parallel that Robert McAlmon, Williams's co-editor on *Contact,* implied in his review of *Kora in Hell,* calling the book "a sort of re-touched photograph."[8]

In his autobiography Williams remembers meeting Duchamp with the "Others" group at Grantwood, and that whenever he attended Arensberg's parties in New York "you always saw Marcel Duchamp there" (*Auto,* 135, 136). He recalls that on one occasion at the Arensbergs' Duchamp snubbed him when he tried to engage the artist in discussion about his *The Sisters* (*Auto,* 137). This work, usually known as *Yvonne and Magdeline Torn in Tatters* (1911), bears some similarities to the Davis frontispiece in *Kora.* Duchamp later wrote of this painting:

> Introducing humor for the first time in my paintings I, so to speak, tore up their profiles and placed them at random on the canvas. You can see four profiles floating in mid-air. There again we have a very loose interpretation of the cubist theories— two profiles of each sister of a different scale and scattered about the canvas; in other words, I was trying very hard to get away from any traditional or even cubistic composition.[9]

As in the Davis drawing, traditional perspective is destroyed for the artist's own creative purpose. This kind of work presaged Duchamp's extension of the idea into his ready-mades. There, in the words of the *Blind Man* editorial, "He took an ordinary article of life [the urinal], placed it so that its useful significance disappeared under the new title and point of view—created a new thought for that object."[10] Williams similary sought to deprive conventional word patterns of their "useful significance," and to use words in the new context of his own choosing. One of the improvisations, number XXI, I, following the dictum "A poem can be made of anything" in the preceding passage, offers speculations on a bathtub, and a commentary that concludes: "There is nothing in antiquity to equal this" (*Imag,* 71).

The improvisations appear to be in random order, but it is our expectations of a *particular* order that allows Williams his effect of novelty. Similarly with Duchamp, the everyday nature of the objects that become ready-mades sets up a tension between use and presentation, the practical and the imaginative, mass production and the unique construct.

This play with expectation also lay behind the painters' and poets' interest in the visual dimension of printed language. Our habitual response to language is temporal and associative. As part of their strategy to break up the conventions of representation, the cubist artists incorporated words and individual letters into their compositions. A fragment from a newspaper might form part of a collage, setting up a tension between the previous context of mass communication and the present context of the fragment's specific use in a unique work. Or a word or series of letters might be stencilled onto the canvas. The words in the painting would often teasingly suggest some commentary upon an aspect of the work, but the viewer's semantic expectations would finally have to give way to recognizing the function of the letters as a compositional element, acknowledging their formal function as shape. In the improvisations the layout of nonitalicized passages, italicized commentaries, and ruled lines also form visual patterns that run counter to our expectations of linear narrative sequence.

In his "Prologue" Williams cites Duchamp's assertion that "a stained-glass window that had fallen out and lay more or less together on the ground was of far greater interest than the thing conventionally composed *in situ*" (*Imag,* 8). Part of this "greater interest" comes from the play of chance and composition in this "descended" window, but the comment also points to the attention modernist artists paid to glass as a medium. The German expressionists produced paintings upon glass, and Marsden Hartley experimented with the medium in the years 1917 through 1919. But the most famous glass composition of its day was Duchamp's *The Bride Stripped Bare by Her Bachelors, Even* (1915–23). Art historian Milton Brown has commented:

> These glass constructions consisted of abstract compositions in paint and metal foil, contrived with meticulous mechanical precision upon panes of glass. The result was a window or transparent screen which might be viewed as an isolated abstract pattern or, when placed within a room, as a sort of foreground frame behind which shifting haphazard groupings would create continually changing pictures. In his earlier experiments, Duchamp was preoccupied with esthetic construction, but in these glass compositions there was for a time a balance between the rational aspects of artistic manipulation, from which he was soon to turn, and the irrational nature of chance into which, with perverse logic, he was subsequently to move.[11]

In his autobiography Williams recalls seeing the glass at Arensberg's apartment (*Auto,* 136). The work might possibly be that "complexity with a surface of glass" of Improvisation XXVII, I, that is specifically associated with poetry.

> The particular thing . . . offers a finality that sends us spinning through space, a fixity the mind could climb forever, a revolving mountain, a complexity with a surface of glass; the gist of poetry (*Imag,* 81).

Glass becomes a frequent metaphor in Williams's work from this time forward. Sometimes the metaphor functions as the barrier that separates the artist from the "inventive imagination." At other times, as in the improvisation above, it becomes the slivered material of a poem born out of the breaking of that barrier. In March 1919 he titled a series of poems in *Poetry* "Broken Windows." Behind Williams's interest lay not only the particular compositions he might have seen on glass, but also the modern painters' strategy of rejecting the traditional idea of a painting as a naturalistic view through a framed window. One way the painters set about this was to incorporate the frame into the picture—painting the frame, as Hartley did in some of his Berlin pictures. (In some of his later poems Williams similarly incorporated his title into the poem itself.) Another device was to utilize the window motif in a composition uncompromisingly two-dimensional, as in Hartley's *A Bermuda Window in a Semi-Tropic Character* or Juan Gris' *The Open Window.*

In Williams's work at this time, the glass barrier that the artist must break through is sometimes presented as the windshield of a car transporting the poet and his roving eye. This is the case with the 1919 "Romance Moderne" (*CEP,* 181–84) a poem which it is particularly useful to examine in the context of the improvisations. The poem begins with a description, strong in vivid movement, of the world the poet senses outside his car.

> Tracks of rain and light linger in
> the spongy greens of a nature whose
> flickering mountain—bulging nearer,
> ebbing back into the sun
> hollowing itself away to hold a lake,—
> or brown stream rising and falling
> at the roadside, turning about,
> churning itself white, drawing
> green in over it,—plunging glassy funnels
> fall—

But the poet and his companion are trapped in "the other world— / the windshield a blunt barrier." The "first desire is / to fling oneself out at the side into / the other dance, to other music," a violent movement that would release "the *unseen* power of words" (my emphasis). The release of this power requires the exercise of sight, not the perusal of dictionaries.

The only way to join "the other dance," to release "the unseen power of words," is to take a "new direction": the route the improvisations take to "let the imagination have its own way to see if it can save itself".

> Lean forward. Punch the steersman
> behind the ear. Twirl the wheel!
> Over the edge! Screams! Crash!

> The end. I sit above my head—
> a little removed—or
> a thin wash of rain on the roadway
> —I am never afraid when he is driving,—
> interposes new direction,
> rides us sidewise, unforseen
> into the ditch! All threads cut!
> Death! Black. The end. The very end—

The "blunt barrier" is now broken. The poet's "emotions" are "blind"—cut off from habitual associations—but now, "stirred, the eye seizes / for the first time—The eye awake!" The poem can now parallel the manifold patterns behind the dance of nature, "the unseen power of words" bringing the energy to language that matches a world perceived without the imposition of conventions of order.

> And the white moon already up.
> White. Clean. All the colors.
> A good head, backed by the eye—awake!
> backed by the emotions—blind—
> River and mountain, light and rain—or
> rain, rock, light, trees—divided:
> rain-light counter rocks—trees or
> trees counter rain-light-rocks or—
>
> Myriads of counter processions

In the "Prologue" Williams cites Kandinsky's axioms for the artist.

> Every artist has to express himself.
> Every artist has to express his epoch.
> Every artist has to express the pure and eternal
>   qualities of the art of all men.
>
> (*Imag*, 26)

Since Williams quotes a shortened form of Wadsworth's *Blast* translation, it remains problematic whether he had read the complete *Ueber das Geistige in der Kunst* at this time. But whether Williams was familiar with the complete book or not, Kandinsky's views received wide enough discussion in the press and magazines for an interested reader to become aware of his chief ideas. An art historian has recently pointed out that "one could, in 1914, learn of Kandinsky's ideas simply by reading the newspaper."[12] In addition, Pound had endorsed Kandinsky's ideas, and Marsden Hartley (who, according to John Cournos, could talk at length "with extreme lucidity about modern art")[13] was now back in the United States from Berlin, passing the winter and spring of 1916 in New York. As his glass paintings of the period indicate, The Blaue Reiter school remained a potent influence upon his work. Williams's citation of Kandinsky in the "Prologue" is part of the same long sentence that quotes from an Adobe Indian song. While in Berlin, Hartley expressed the "inner necessity" of his American spirit through a number of paintings based upon American Indian symbols.

Williams almost certainly borrowed his term "improvisation" from Kandinsky. In his treatise Kandinsky defined an "Impression," an "Improvisation," and a "Composition".

1. A direct impression of outward nature, expressed in purely artistic form. This I call an "Impression."
2. A largely unconscious, spontaneous expression of inner character, the non-material nature. This I call an "Improvisation."
3. An expression of slowly formed inner feeling, which comes to utterance only after long maturing. This I call a "Composition". In this, reason, consciousness, purpose, play an overwhelming part. But of the calculation nothing appears, only the feeling.[14]

The only example of Kandinsky's own "Improvisations" that Williams had probably seen was *Improvisation No. 27,* Kandinsky's sole exhibit at the Armory Show, subsequently purchased by Stieglitz. Kandinsky's work was not shown again in the U.S. until the fifth exhibition of the Société Anonyme in 1920. In A. J. Eddy's ground-breaking study *Cubists and Post-Impressionism* (1914) Williams could have seen reproductions of two further *Improvisations,* numbers 29 and 30. In his book Eddy considers Kandinsky the major modernist painter, and devotes considerable attention to his work, all of which he calls, somewhat misleadingly, "Improvisations." Eddy's treatment of Kandinsky's *Improvisations* as a very pure example of compositional painting"[15] (Eddy's emphasis) is closer to Williams intent in *Kora in Hell* than Kandinsky's own separation of the term from "Composition" and "Impression." In Eddy's discussion, as in *Kora in Hell,* the emphasis falls upon fusing the spontaneity of personal expression with the harmony of composed form.

Hartley wrote to Williams praising the structure of the improvisations in terms that suggest the application of Kandinsky. He found a "beautiful plasticity in the book," and acknowledged that the improvisations "have a gift for real spiritual geometric in them."[16]

For Kandinsky, the patterns of mathematics manifested the "hidden form" beneath the personal expression of his art. Herbert Read has summarized the painter's position:

Kandinsky was always conscious of the mathematical basis of form, "The final abstract expression of every art is number," he declared with emphasis in his book, and for this reason if for no other he could not finally surrender himself to any form of automatism. The work of art must have a "hidden construction"; not an obvious geometrical construction, but nevertheless one with "calculated effects."[17]

This "hidden construction," Kandinsky wrote in *The Art of Spiritual Harmony,* could be expressed in "irregular" mathematical form.

This "concealed construction" may arise from an apparently fortuitous selection of forms on the canvas. Their external lack of cohesion is their internal harmony. This haphazard arrangement of forms may be the future of artistic harmony. Their fundamental relationship will finally be able to be expressed in mathematical form, but in terms irregular rather than regular.[18]

Kandinsky could consequently write to A. J. Eddy "that the element of chance is very rarely met with in these [i.e. his own] pictures."[19]

Williams declared in *Spring and All* that "it is necessary to dwell in the imagination if the truth is to be numbered" (*Imag*, 112). In both *Spring and All* and *Kora in Hell* the "imagination" is "numbered" in twenty-seven sections. In *Kora in Hell* there is no apparent pattern behind how many italicized or nonitalicized passages appear in any particular section, but the sections are regularly broken down into units numbered 1, 2 and 3 (a pattern made "irregular" by the exception of XI). Thus the numerical relationship of each unit to its section mirrors the numerical relationship of each section to the overall pattern of twenty-seven—3 × 3 × 3 yielding the product 27. In their common interlocking quality the numerical units reveal their "concealed construction." The relationship of factor to product emphasizes the self-referential nature of the book's form—its own "inner necessity"—while the recurrence of threes in the patterning denies the importance of numerical progression, matching the cyclical themes of the work. The resulting uniformity of emphasis parallels the Davis frontispiece and Williams's assertion that "all things have their perfections."

Williams may have settled on the number three because it is the least number on which a pattern may be formed. But he probably knew of Duchamp's experiments to coordinate the effects of chance with a patterning of threes in his *Network of Stoppages* (1914). The number may also reflect an aspect of Williams's constant theme of transforming the past into a present vitality. Behind the threes of "On Gay Wallpaper" (1928) John Dixon Hunt has detected the invocation of traditional iconography.[20]

And on this moral sea
of grass or dreams lie flowers
or baskets of desires

Heaven knows what they are
between cerulean shapes
laid regularly round

Mat roses and tridentate
leaves of gold
threes, threes and threes
(*CEP*, 345)

The number twenty-seven not only has a special mathematical relationship with three, it is the number of the only Kandinsky *Improvisation*
that Williams had probably seen. Twenty-seven was also important to
Marsden Hartley, whose prose and Berlin paintings document his invest-
ing certain numbers with a mystical significance. Twenty-seven was the
number of Gertrude Stein's residence in Paris, and the painter told her
in a letter: "I have somewhat the same feeling toward the number 27 that
I have toward 291—they both have a magic of their own."[21] When Hartley recalled the 291 gallery in his *Adventures in the Arts* as "on Fifth
Avenue near Twenty-seventh Street" he was finding the gallery's closeness to Twenty-seventh Street more significant than its actual location
between Thirtieth and Thirty-first![22]

At the same time that Williams in the "Prologue" aligns his sense of the
necessary "inventive imagination" with the innovations in contemporary
painting, he takes issue with those poets who he feels have failed to
respond adequately to the contemporary need for change. In "America,
Whitman, and the Art of Poetry" he describes Wallace Stevens, T. S.
Eliot, Ezra Pound, and John Gould Fletcher as "going over the forms of
yesterday," while even Kreymborg and Maxwell Bodenheim come in for
criticism.[23] In the "Prologue," however, the inadequacy of Stevens, Eliot,
Pound, and the "Mid-West" poets is set against the innovative work of
Williams's "Others" colleagues, Kreymborg (although with reservations),
Bodenheim, Marianne Moore, and Mina Loy. Behind these demarcations
the various writers become another example of those "two contending
forces" (*Imag*, 32) in *Kora in Hell*, out of which, as in the balance of
forms in a painting, the composition itself is defined.

The initial impulse to quote from personal letters in the "Prologue"
may have come from Williams's annoyance at Pound. A reference in one
of Pound's letters suggests that Williams had taken exception to Pound's
quoting in print from their personal correspondence (possibly this from

The Little Review for October 1917: "An American author writes to me 'You mix your damn foolery with sense, so you continue readable'"). Pound retorted in November:

> My dear William: At what date did you join the ranks of the old ladies? Among the male portion of the community one constantly uses fragments of letters, fragments of conversation (anonymously, quite anonymously, NOT referring to the emitter by name) for the purpose of sharpening a printed argument.[24]

Williams takes up the practice, but true to the spirit of the improvisations, he ignores the conventional proprieties. But he appears to have soon regretted it, to judge by a letter from Hartley in which the painter writes, "I think with you that the Prologue is a little showy and intimate."[25]

In later years Williams remembered that T. S. Eliot's "Prufrock" appeared "when I was halfway through the 'Prologue'" (*IWWP*, 30). But the "Prologue" is dated 1 September 1918, and *Prufrock and Other Observations* was published in London in June 1917 (while Williams was writing the improvisations). Nevertheless, his erroneous recollection testifies to the impact that Eliot's growing influence and reputation had on him while he was writing the "Prologue." What he may specifically have been remembering is either the four Eliot poems that appeared in *The Little Review* in September 1918, or, more probably, the article by Edgar Jepson in support of Eliot that appeared in the same issue. Jepson's *Little Review* article, "The Western School," is a shortened version of his "Recent United States Poetry" from *The English Review* of May 1918. The article is a complaint against *Poetry*'s prize poets Frost, Masters, and Lindsay, and in the "Prologue" Williams grants that "his epithets and praises . . . are in the main well-merited" (*Imag*, 23). His objection to Jepson's article is that Eliot is held up as a praiseworthy alternative.

Although Eliot's definitive essay "Tradition and the Individual Talent" did not appear in *The Egoist* until 1919, his attitude towards tradition was clear from his numerous articles and reviews in the magazine. In his review of Harriet Monroe's anthology *The New Poetry* (which included seven poems by Williams), he declared:

> We cannot change much; the point is to do a good job where we can. In literature especially, the innovations which we can consciously and collectively aim to introduce are few, and mostly technical. The main thing is to be quite certain what these are.

For Eliot, those writers in the anthology who had managed to avoid rhetoric and find a mode of expression differing from that of the previous generation had done so by a careful, reasoned understanding of emotional and artistic nuance, "by the exercise, in greater or less degree, of intelligence, of which an important function is the discernment of exactly what, and how much, we feel in any given situation."[26]

This degree of self-consciousness runs counter to the emphasis in *Kora in Hell* upon novelty and spontaneity. As Williams's account in the "Prologue" of his mother losing her way in Rome makes clear, the only way to see "the thing itself," divorced from past associations, is "without forethought or afterthought but with great intensity of perception" (*Imag,* 8). While Eliot sought to introduce technical innovation into an existing array of forms, Williams demanded an "inventive imagination" that would produce new forms equal to those the painters had developed to express a new way of seeing.

Williams scoffs in the "Prologue" at Eliot's poem "La Figlia Che Piange": "it adds to the pleasant outlook from the club window" (*Imag,* 25). His chief complaints against the poem are its self-consciousness— "just the right amount of everything drained through . . . the rhythm delicately studied"—and its conformity. In its last stanza, Williams argues, it moves from "conscious simplicity" to "absolute unintelligibility" through "the inevitable straining after a rhyme" (*Imag,* 25). Williams had no objection to unintelligibility, arguing in 1919 that "Americans are cursed with a desire to be understood" (*ARI,* 60). But Eliot's "conscious simplicity" was already the imposition of thought upon words, and his "unintelligibility" no result of the difficulty of expression, but merely a botched conformity to an external rhyme scheme.

Williams's attitude toward innovation is that of Duchamp and "the great masters of antiquity"—the compositional pattern stems from recognizing "that diversity of context in things" (*Imag,* 48). "Thus by a mere twist of the imagination, if Prufrock only knew it, the whole world can be inverted" (*Imag,* 25). And Williams's attitude toward the artist's obligation to tradition mirrors Kandinsky's. His citation of Kandinsky's axioms in the "Prologue" immediately follows this discussion of Eliot. Kandinsky's position (here summarized by Eddy) would have met with Williams's complete approval.

A man may so steep himself in history and tradition that all he does is reminiscent of the past, but such work marks no progress and such men are negligible factors in the advancement of mankind.

It is the man who yields himself to *his times,* who absorbs all there is of good in the *life about him,* who sees everything, who mingles with his respect for the achievements of the past a mighty admiration for the triumphs of the present—such a man is a leader among his fellows; brilliant thinker, daring adventurer, he blazes the way for the timid to follow.[27]

In reaction to what Pound and Eliot saw as the flaccidity of *vers libre*, their work became more allusive and tighter in structure in these years. Together they advocated the virtues of French verse. Eliot wrote some poems in the language, issues of *The Egoist* and *The Little Review* were given over to French poetry, and Pound praised the fact that Laforgue "writes not the popular language of any country but an international tongue common to the excessively cultivated, and to those more or less familiar with French literature of the first three-fourths of the nineteenth century."[28] Eliot utilized the quatrains of Gautier and the internal rhymes of Laforgue, while Pound's experiments included a neoclassical satire, "L'Homme Moyen Sensual" (rejected by Williams for *Others*) and the Troubador poems "Homage a Langue D'Oc" and "Near Perigord."

In "America, Whitman, and the Art of Poetry" Williams also demanded a structure behind *vers libre*. "Free verse merely means verse whose proper structure escapes a man's efforts to control it." His call to discipline can even sound like Eliot's: "The only freedom a poet can have is to be conscious of his manoevres, to recognize whither he is tending and to govern his sensibilities, his mind, his will so that it accords delicately with his emotions." But Williams rejects the possibility of finding such an 'accord' in the "aristocratic forms" of "pentameters, hexameters and . . . quatrains."

> But back of these aristocratic forms lies the democratic groundwork of all forms, basic elements that can be comprehended and used with new force. Being far back in the psychic history of all races no flavor of any certain civilization clings to them, they remain and will remain forever universal, to be built with freely by him who can into whatever perfections he is conscious of. It is here that we must seek.[29]

In the "Prologue" Williams argues that expression of the American "accord" requires the kind of open-ended patterning that characterizes the improvisations. Pound and Eliot's emphasis upon balance and "discernment" results in their work's remaining wedded to anachronistic forms. Pound is characterized as speaking "like a Frenchman," and as "one who discerns." Consequently, "the accordances of which Americans have the parts and the colors but not the completions before them pass beyond the attempts of his thought" (*Imag,* 27).

For Williams, the imposition of "discernment" would place an artificial restraint upon expression, killing the "fool" who is such an important voice in the improvisations. The Bacchanalian "fool" can discover new contexts for language (one version of this theme in the improvisations is the "four rollicking companions," of improvisation XI who have "evaded the stringent laws of the country") (*Imag, 52*). Williams's objections in the "Prologue" to H. D. and to Wallace Stevens are in terms of their failure to allow this "fool" expression. He argues that H. D.—now with *The Egoist*—misses the importance of the "hey-ding-ding touch" in his poem "March": the "touch [that] is the prototype of the Improvisations" (*Imag, 13*). Her application of the term "sacred" to literature is an anachronism (unlike, Williams could have said, Fra Angelico's 'timeless' treatment of a sacred subject in his *Annunciation*).

Williams prints a letter from Wallace Stevens in the "Prologue," in which Stevens, responding to *Al Que Quiere!*, advocates the thorough exploration of a single perspective.

> My idea is that in order to carry a thing through to the extreme necessity to convey it one has to stick to it. . . . Given a fixed point of view, realistic, imagistic or what you will, everything adjusts itself to that point of view; and the process of adjustment is a world in flux, as it should be for a poet. But to fidget with points of view leads always to new beginnings and incessant new beginnings lead to sterility (*Imag, 15*).

Stevens's strategy offers itself and is rejected in an early improvisation. The passage did not appear in *The Little Review* extracts, and was probably added to reflect upon the Stevens's letter in the "Prologue" (there is an added reference to Stevens's exotic tastes).

> Why go further? One might conceivably rectify the rhythm, study all out and arrive at the perfection of a tiger lily or a china doorknob. One might lift all out of the ruck, be a worthy successor to—the man in the moon. Instead of breaking the back of a willing phrase why not try to follow the wheel through—approach death at a walk, take in all the scenery. There's as much reason one way as the other and then—one never knows—perhaps we'll bring back Eurydice—this time! (*Imag, 32*).

But the inadequacy of this approach is made clear in the next improvisation: "*Ay dio.* I would say so much were it not for the tunes changing, changing, darting so many ways. One step and the cart's left you sprawling" (*Imag, 33*).

For Williams, it was only by fidgeting "with points of view," as the modern painters had done, that a poem could achieve an autonomous existence. The way to discover and exploit "the unseen power of words" in a poem was to approach the work of art from so many different perspectives that no one set of relationships or associations could impose its own pattern. Imagination should master analysis and habitual association: "Given many things of nearly totally divergent natures but possessing one-thousandth part of a quality in common, provided that be new, distinguished, these things belong in an imaginative category and not in a gross natural array" (*Imag,* 14). The poem was that "imaginative category" for words, as a painting such as the Davis frontispiece in *Kora in Hell* was the "imaginative category" for the painter's multiple perspectives of Gloucester. When an "imaginative category" captured that "one-thousandth part of a quality in common," then for Williams it possessed a "reality" as real as anything in nature. The American poet or painter had to search for those "parts and . . . colors" which were "the accordances" of his own environment. And when successful, he not only created a reality as real as nature, but, as Kandinsky insisted, the problem of the relationship of his work to tradition became an irrelevance; "On this level all things and ages meet in fellowship" (*Imag,* 27, 19). For Stevens, however, the interrelations of language, form, and environment remained problematical. A poem was one exploration of a possible solution, or the discovery of the impossibility of a solution, certainly not a captured moment of synthesis.

To those writers who advocate analysis and discernment Williams opposes his "Others" colleagues. In his praise of Marianne Moore, he again advocates feeling before reason. Her limitation of subject matter is not the result of despair or discernment, but stems from an "austerity of mood"—the mood generated by the passion of the moralist (*Imag,* 10). Maxwell Bodenheim, whose visual orientation Williams dramatized in *Al Que Quiere!*'s "M. B.", receives unqualified approval in the "Prologue." Three lines of his "Chorus Girl" (from *Minna and Myself*) introduce the essay, and Williams later praises this "heroic figure" for his "self-absorption" and the private nature of his work (*Imag,* 27).

Kreymborg's poetry of "transforming music" meets with Williams's only limited approval. But he is at any rate an "innovator" and a perceptive editor. In a passage that appeared only in *The Little Review* version of the "Prologue," Williams wrote that "Kreymborg believes in the power of music upon words to transform them," but that "Alfred has little help from the eyes."[30] Concentration upon music led Kreymborg to retain and even emphasize many effects of language that Williams eschewed in his own work, such as rhetorical tropes and alliteration. His "Prose Rhythms, 1906" come close to the style of Williams's improvisations, but their concern with sound as theme and technique causes them to lack that "loose linking" Williams demanded of innovative form.[31]

In keeping with the painterly orientation of the "Prologue," Williams concludes the essay with praise for his friend Demuth. After Demuth's summer with Hartley in Provincetown in 1917 his work incorporated the influence of Cézanne. He distorted perspective and developed his "ray line" technique to emphasize the line as the basic unit of composition. Between 1916 and 1918 he painted many vaudeville studies, combining a quintessential American subject with an interest in the "fool". The painter is himself prepared to be the "fool"—he drinks not for the taste of the liquor, but for "the effect it [has] on his mind" (*Imag*, 28). In also treating the American industrial landscape as subject matter for painting, and breaking its utilitarian structures down into linear compositional elements, Demuth displayed the "knowledge of that diversity of context in things" (*Imag*, 48) that Williams demanded of the "inventive imagination." And his watercolor studies of flowers (Williams purchased one, *Pink Lady Slippers*, in the year he wrote the "Prologue") display a similar interest in "diversity of context". Williams told Emily Farnham that in this painting Demuth "was interested in the similarity between the forms of the flowers and the phallic symbol, the male genitals."[32]

Responding to the work of such artists as Davis, Duchamp, Kandinsky and Demuth, Williams achieved in *Kora in Hell: Improvisations* an innovative, complexly patterned work ; a form that is alive to contemporary conditions and is rooted both in personal expression and a universal mythic pattern. The language is the artist's own while uncompromisingly part of the self-referential nature of the artifact. Williams had achieved a resolution that he would build upon in the poems of *Sour Grapes*, and the multidirectional patterns within the prose and poems of *Spring and All*.

1. Wassily Kandinsky, *Improvisation No. 27*, 1912. Oil on canvas, 47³/₈″ x 55¹/₄″. The Metropolitan Museum of Art, The Alfred Steiglitz Collection, 1949.

2. Marsden Hartley. *Painting No. 5,* 1914-15. Oil on canvas, 100.3 x 80.6 cm. Whitney Museum of American Art, New York. Cover illustration for *Marsden Hartley* by Barbara Haskell, 1980. This painting, memorializing the death of a German military officer friend of the artist at the beginning of World War I, was painted in Berlin and included in an exhibition devoted to Hartley's work in Berlin in 1915.

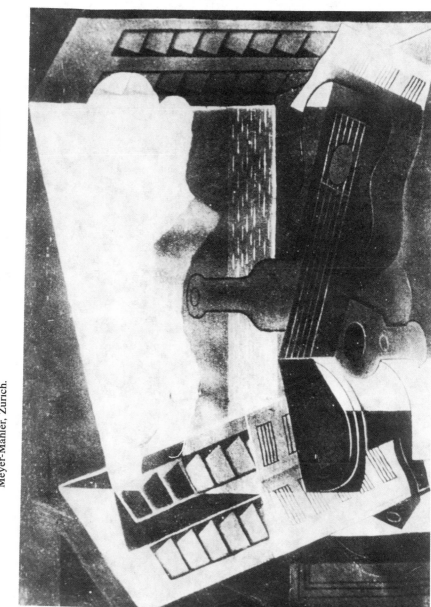

4. Juan Gris. *The Open Window*, 1921. Oil on canvas, 25¾" x 39½". Collection M. Meyer-Mahler, Zurich.

3. Marsden Hartley. *New Mexico Landscape*, 1919-20. Oil on canvas, 76.2 x 91.4 cm. (30" x 36"). Philadelphia Museum of Art, The Alfred Steiglitz Collection.

5. Charles Demuth. *Tuberoses*, 1922. Watercolor on paper, 13⁹/₁₆″ x 11⁵/₈.
   Private collection.

6. Charles Sheeler. *Interior*, 1926. Oil on canvas, 33″ x 22″. Whitney Museum of American Art, New York.

5

Sour Grapes

The years 1919 through 1921 were very productive for Williams. Although *Others* folded after he edited the final issue in July 1919, by December 1920 he had cofounded a successor, *Contact,* with a new associate, Robert McAlmon. By the summer of the following year they had produced four issues. In addition to this activity, his *Kora in Hell: Improvisations* appeared in September 1920, and a book of verse, *Sour Grapes,* in December of the following year.

Williams met McAlmon through Marsden Hartley, and in *Contact* the two men campaigned aggressively for American art of international standards. Williams had been moving towards this "local" position since *Al Que Quiere!* but his rhetoric intensified with the exodus to Europe— once the war ended—of the New York based avant-garde artists, both European and American. By the time *Sour Grapes* appeared even McAlmon and Hartley were in Europe. Williams remembered the mood of the volume as one of "disappointment, sorrow. I felt rejected by the world" (*IWWP,* 33–34). This mood probably accounts for the last-minute change of title from *Picture Poems,* but many of the poems are written in a more positive spirit than the title would suggest.

In her study of Hartley, Barbara Haskell sums up the strategy of those American artists who remained behind, faced with the spectacle of the scramble to Europe.

> [Hartley] wrote that Spring to Harriet Monroe of his preference for recognizable objective images, asserting that all art was moving back to realism. In this, Hartley was very much of his time: the American sense of disillusionment and isolationism that followed the war manifested itself artistically in a general retreat from abstraction and a return to more representational modes. As the cynicism about American participation in European affairs grew, involvement with European painting was supplanted by the desire to identify what was American and what constituted the American spirit.[1]

But within this American emphasis, Williams's demand in *Contact* was always for work that matched international, not provincial, modernist standards. Both Williams and McAlmon inveighed against the provincialism of the Midwest prairie school of poets. In one of the first letters between the two men McAlmon declares that he is now quite alone in the city: "and I don't love humanity, or Sandburg, or give a tinker's damn about the spiritual voice of America." He had heard enough of this "voice" from Waldo Frank at a recent party. "By the time they had shoveled enough of the above shit into my ears regarding the growth of voices that are American in the one way, naturally, that one can be, Windy, Whitmanesque, and mental masturbatory, I decided I'd better get in touch with you again."[2]

Reviewing *Kora in Hell* in the April 1921 *Poetry*, McAlmon argued that Williams had found another way to be "American." McAlmon's language has echoes of Kandinsky's. Masters, Sandburg, and Aiken "either write verse yearning for a pastoral America now long gone," or they churn out "sweep-of-the-corn-sap-flowing rhythms." Either way, their approach does not develop "into a more spiritual type of searching." Behind the forces they extol "are more fundamental forces which they do not sense, forces which have a universal application, while retaining also a strictly local significance. The experience of the locality is after all that of the universe. The history of an individual relates itself with startling similarity to that of the age." Williams's *Kora in Hell*, McAlmon concludes, is unique in rejecting "logic, sequence, order," and thus being "vividly aware of age conceptions, qualities, colors, noises, and philosophies."[3]

Williams wrote in *Contact*, "In exploiting his position in America the artist, aware of the universal physical laws of his craft, will however take off only from the sensual accidents of his immediate contacts." Williams's emphasis is now upon these "immediate contacts." The "general conditions" of the American environment "form the only unity we possess. On this basis alone can we afford dispersion of efforts, the modern individualistic dispersion" (*ARI*, 67). Thus, although Williams still acknowledges Kandinsky to be "a great artist," his greatness is that he expresses "skillfully the seething reactions of the contemporary European consciousness" (*Imag*, 173). The lesson Matisse offers in painting a reclining nude "with interest in the place she had chosen" is how he captured a "french girl" in "the french sun, on the french grass" (*SE*, 30–31).

Contact was to provide a basis for the "dispersion of efforts" of the painters and poets interested in "immediate contacts," painting and poetry being the two forms that most interested Williams, Hartley, and McAlmon. These are the terms in which McAlmon describes the genesis of the magazine in his autobiographical novel *Post-Adolescence* (1923). After a stimulating discussion with the painter Brander Ogden (Hartley),

Peter (McAlmon himself) meets Jim Boyle (Williams) at a hospital in the city. Peter tells him, "I have some ideas in my head about getting writers and painters together. It's got to be done in this country; nobody else will help them if they don't help each other . . ." Jim replies, "I don't get this modern art at all, but I can't find the terms with which to condemn it either. Tradition doesn't satisfy. We haven't any base at all."[4]

In its five issues the material in *Contact* included two Wallace Gould poems titled "Lithographs," Marianne Moore's "In the Days of Prismatic Color," "Patterns" by Virgil Jordan, Williams's essay "A Matisse," McAlmon on Dada, and some prose and poetry of Hartley's. In addition, the magazine devoted a good deal of space to one of Hartley's discoveries, the painter Rex Slinkard (1887–1918). Issues one, two, and three carried selections from his letters, and issues one and three reproductions of his paintings.

Hartley wrote an introduction, "Rex Slinkard, Ranchman and Poet-Painter," for an exhibition of Slinkard's work in Los Angeles, the piece reappearing in the catalog for a 1920 show at the Knoedler gallery in New York. McAlmon was equally impressed with Slinkard, and wrote to Williams in 1921 contrasting the painter's work with the writings of Williams's new friend Kenneth Burke.

> Slinkard—whether one likes him or not, and I do, seeing that it is young, blind religious instinct as was Whitman's, I still like him—and it is because he was feeling for life, out to discover—and to hell with art as an ideal—the only way Burke sees it: a means of evading experience.[5]

Slinkard's letters are characterized by a sensuous, self-conscious response to the Western landscape, and careful, detailed descriptions of his Spartan living conditions. Writing in *Contact,* Williams titled one of his own central statements of the "contact" ethic, "Yours O Youth," out of these letters. "What is it I see in Rex Slinkard's letters?" he asks. "It is all very young, this man's writing about his painting; it is what I recognize as in some measure definitely and singularly American" (*SE,* 34). In the essay Williams describes the literary results of "contact" in painterly terms.

> Contact always implies a local definition of effort with a consequent taking on of certain colors from the locality by the experience, and these colors or sensual values of whatever sort are the only realities in writing or, as may be said, the essential quality in literature (*SE,* 32).

The poet's act of contact incorporates the "certain colors" that come out of his careful observation into a pattern expressive of the self, the locale, and the universal. Many of the *Sour Grapes* poems are organized around color. In "Daisy" (*CEP*, 208) the common flower becomes "The dayseye hugging the earth," the poet as sun (a frequent motif in *Al Que Quiere!*) now one with the concrete object. This motif of light and vision becomes the center around which the colors of the poem coalesce: "Purple," "black," "green," "brownedged / green and pointed scales," and the "greenfastened" petals unite "round the yellow center," as "he sends out / his twenty rays." "Primrose" (*CEP*, 209) begins with the assertion that "Yellow, yellow, yellow, yellow! . . . is not a color." It is again the realization of "sensual values," that here unites "a bluebird," "blue paper," "a threecluster of / green walnuts swaying," "a man / swinging his pink fists," "five red petals," "a red stem six feet high," and the "tufts of purple grass" that "spot the green meadow." In "The Disputants" the "violent disarray" of rooted color is "composed" through the poet's careful observation and patterning. The result is a "picture poem" that reads very much like a verbal transcription of a still-life.

> Upon the table in their bowl!
> in violent disarray
> of yellow sprays, green spikes
> of leaves, red pointed petals
> and curled heads of blue
> and white among the litter
> of the forks and crumbs and plates
> the flowers remain composed.
> Coolly their colloquy continues
> above the coffee and loud talk
> grown frail as vaudeville.
>
> (*CEP*, 218)

But although the theory of contact is obviously useful as a way of reading Williams's work, as a critical theory it suffers from the same deficiencies as those theories of art that are its source. The purpose behind the theories of Worringer, and his forbears Riegl, Dvořák, and Sedlmayr, in stressing intention before skill, was to provide a rationale for abstract art.[6] Egyptian, Byzantine and modern art were unrealistic not because of the artists' inability to reproduce nature, but because of a deliberate artistic intent—an intent linked to the "spirit of the race" and the understood needs of the times. But the theory of contact argues for a kind of sensibility that is peculiarly American, and also for distinctions between levels of achievement. The compromise is an uneasy one, and more usefully serves as a strategy by which Williams can reject, for example, the "Windy" prairie poets, than as a consistent critical theory. Time has not shown Rex Slinkard's work, for example, to be a lasting force in American art; he appears in no important histories, and is rarely mentioned even in comprehensive dictionaries of American artists. Williams overpraised Alfred Kreymborg and Maxwell Bodenheim, and was often uncomfortable with the achievements of Pound and Eliot. Although he praises the iconoclasm of "Others" colleague Emanuel Carnevali, Williams concedes "Carnevali has not written three poems I can thoroughly admire . . . his poems are bad, full of nonsense."[7] Nevertheless, Williams dedicated the final issue of *Others* to him.

Similarly, it was for Wallace Gould's method, rather than his achievement, that Williams and Hartley together publicized him in the pages of *Poetry* and *The Little Review*. Like McAlmon and Slinkard, Gould was a protégé of Hartley's. He came from Hartley's own state of Maine, and had published *Children of the Sun: Rhapsodies and Poems* in 1917, as well as several poems in *The Little Review, Others* and *The Seven Arts*. His book received a long review from Harriet Monroe in the October 1918 *Poetry,* where she comments, "Recently Mr. Marsden Hartley reproached me for neglecting it." Although less than enthusiastic herself, she quotes Hartley's remark that Gould achieves "the elimination of personal interpretation" since "his voice is as authentic as the life of the place itself."[8] Hartley characterized the poet in *The Little Review* the following year as "the voice of Maine in modern poetry."[9] In a postscript, the magazine's editor, Margaret Anderson, protested praising a writer for his approach rather than for his achievement. She similarly objected the following month to Williams's article "A Maker" in support of Hartley and Gould. Williams, who published Gould in *Others* and later in *Contact,* distinguished the Maine poet from "the lovely singers of the plains" by his "quiet scorn." "He sticks to what he sees, what he knows, but the quiet scorn of his music has set him free." But Williams wants to deny accomplishment as a primary consideration, while also claiming Gould as a "splendid artist".

> I have nowhere said that Gould is a great poet. I wish I could find the material for making such an assertion. I don't know the man's range. I only begin to feel the depth of his intensity, but that he is a splendid artist I declare now as well as I am able.[10]

Gould remained a darling of the local movement throughout the twenties. Paul Rosenfeld devoted twenty pages of his 1928 *By Way of Art* to him, declaring Gould's work more promising "at present than T. S. Eliot, E. E. Cummings, Hart Crane, Marianne Moore and several other of the poets whose muses still hold out hope of issue."[11] Williams himself, reviewing Gould in a 1929 piece for *The Dial,* felt the poet had still to fulfill his earlier promise.[12]

Williams offers a more helpful distinction between the Prairie poets and his notion of contact in his prose *The Great American Novel* (1923). "Attempting to set down the American background" is there compared to "painting the wind." To this, the imaginary French critic with whom the narrator is at this moment arguing replies: "*Mais ça,* are you a plain imbecile? That is a game for children. Why do you not do as so many of your good writers do? Your Edgar Lee Masters, Your Winesburg, Ohio" (*Imag,* 196).

But Williams rejected what he saw as these writers' undisciplined lyricism. To "paint the wind" well suggests his purpose of capturing a unique moment of movement or growth, and setting the moment in the new time of the patterned poem. The phrase also suggests the visual dimension of the poem, words demarcating space, as the modern painters translated space into an integral part of the composition on the canvas. The captured moment must pulsate with the quality of movement, while the immediacy of the contact draws that moment out of temporal sequence. Through immediacy art translates the moment into the vibrant complexities of its artistic pattern.

As Pound early realized, painting has a long history of developing strategies for conveying movement within stillness. E. H. Gombrich has pointed out that the problem of arrested time has long been a concern of painters. "Expression in life and physiognomic impression rest on movement no less than on static symptoms, and art has to compensate for the loss of the time dimension by concentrating all required information into one arrested image."[13] As noted in chapter 4, Williams was drawn to Stuart Davis's montage of Gloucester scenes as a frontispiece to *Kora in Hell: Improvisations* because the drawing provided "an impressionistic view of the simultaneous" (*IWWP,* 29).

The *Sour Grapes* poems abound with various images of stilled movement. But many of the poems are patterned around the explicit image of the impact of wind upon the landscape, for example, "Approach of Winter," "Blizzard," "The Soughing Wind," and "Arrival." "January" matches the theme of *Al Que Quiere!*'s "M. B.": the poet's adherence to his own pattern, and his refusal to directly transcribe nature.

> Again I reply to the triple winds
> running chromatic fifths of derision
> outside my window:
>   Play louder.
> You will not succeed. I am
> bound more to my sentences
> the more you batter at me
> to follow you.

> And the wind,
> as before, fingers perfectly
> its derisive music.
>   (*CEP,* 197)

The notion of "painting the wind" also conveys the elements of surprise and caprice which, after *Kora in Hell: Improvisations,* Williams built into his poetry. On the level of technique this is often through play with the expected word or line break. The spontaneity is captured within the overall pattern of the poem—the composition impressed with the multiple contours of the passing moment as a stilled landscape of twisted trees and uprooted bushes records the passage of a strong wind. The shapes of the landscape freeze the moment of impact as much as a painting or a poem freezes the moment of the artist's patterned expression.

> The half-stripped trees
> struck by a wind together,
> bending all,
> the leaves flutter drily
> and refuse to let go
> or driven like hail
> stream bitterly out to one side
> and fall
> where the salvias, hard carmine,—
> like no leaf that ever was—
> edge the bare garden.
>   ("Approach of Winter," *CEP,* 197)

In 1919 Harriet Monroe reported a conversation with Williams in which he emphasized the role of mood and spontaneity in his poetic. On a trip East she attended an austere gathering for the "Lowell centenary at the Ritz," had "a memorable talk" with "the reticent" Wallace Stevens, and experienced a "stimulating, even irritating" "Others" party, where she met Williams. "Dr. Carlos Williams," the editor writes,

argued for fluidity of technique—an ever-changeful and episodic rhythm—as the only possible expression of an age of cataclysmic change. How absurd is a fixed poetic method, he insisted, when all the world is dashing to pieces around us! We can't finish a poem in the mood we began it with; every sentence, every choicest phrase, is imperiled by the eruption. The poet should yield like a river to changing banks, rocks, precipices—should yield swiftly, easily, in mid-sentence if need be, taking gladly the new form, the new motion. Poetry must be a series of continually shifting experiments, a thing of changing contours, dancing lights, fluid rhythms, if it is to be true to this age of perpetual motion in which we live.[14]

The effect of such "fluidity of technique" is to emphasize the "new" poem as the only referent of its perpetual motion.

Hartley paralleled many of Williams arguments in a 1921 article, "Dissertation on Modern Painting." "It is a matter of direct contact which we have to consider. The thing must be brought clearly to the surface in terms of itself, without cast or shade of the application of extraneous ideas. That should be, and is, it seems to me, the special and peculiar office of modern art: to arrive at a species of purism, native to ourselves in our own concentrated period, to produce the newness of the 'nowness' of individual experience." Hartley's article discloses the roots of the notion of contact in his echoes of Kandinsky and Worringer. "All the great races had a mission to perform. They had race psychology to perfect . . . every form and movement that we make symbolizes a condition in ourselves."[15]

Hartley's New Mexico canvases (1918–20) suggest their "contact" through an anthropomorphic representation of the features of the New Mexico landscape. Paul Rosenfeld described their overt sexuality: "Earth forms fitting into each other like coupling organs; strawberry-pink mountains dotted by fuzzy poison-green shrubs, recalling breasts and wombs of clay."[16] (Not surprisingly, it is Hartley's praise of Wallace Gould that "his sense of place" is "virile.")[17] Williams purchased one of these paintings, *Mountains in New Mexico* (1919), for $105 at the auction Alfred Stieglitz and Mitchell Kennerly arranged for the artist in 1921 to finance his return to Europe. According to his son, Williams "was wont to refer to" the painting "as Marsden's 'breasts'."[18]

Hartley's use of sexual motifs to represent contact is mirrored in a number of the poems of *Sour Grapes,* Williams extend a motif central to *Al Que Quiere!* In "Romance Moderne":

> Men are not friends where it concerns
> a woman. Fighters. Playfellows.
> White round thighs! Youth! Sighs—!
> It's the fillip of novelty. It's—
>
> Mountains. Elephants humping along
> against the sky—indifferent to
> light withdrawing its tattered shreds,
> worn out with embraces. It's
> the fillip of novelty. It's a fire in the blood.
>
> (*CEP,* 183)

"April" celebrates the doctor's anticipation of the sight of the annually fertile "round and perfect thighs / of the Police Sergeant's wife" (*CEP,*

203). At the conclusion of "Daisy" the allusion to "seashell" suggests the ghostly presence of Botticelli's Venus.

> But turn and turn,
> the crisp petals remain
> brief, translucent, greenfastened,
> barely touching at the edges:
> blades of limpid seashell.
>
> (*CEP*, 208)

And in "Queen Anne's Lace":

> Each part
> is a blossom under his touch
> to which the fibres of her being
> stem one by one, each to its end,
> until the whole field is a
> white desire. . . .
>
> (*CEP*, 210)

"Spouts" uses an image of breasts to suggest the fundamental rhythms of nature. The fountain is as patterned as the poem, and equally as responsive to its source—to the integrity of the internal pressures that inform its shape.

> In this world of
> as fine a pair of breasts
> as ever I saw
> the fountain in
> Madison Square
> spouts up of water
> a white tree
> that dies and lives
> as the rocking water
> in the basin
> turns from the stonerim
> back upon the jet
> and rising there
> reflectively drops down again.
>
> (*CEP*, 222)

In his call for art that expressed the American spirit, Hartley explored other sources of contact. He wrote a number of essays on American Indian culture (the title of a January 1920 essay in *Art and Archaeology*, "Red Man Ceremonials: An American Plea for American Esthetics," is characteristic). Hartley called for comprehension of the "sources" of contemporary expression. "We derive our particular art psychology from definite sources, and it is in comprehension of these sources, and not in the imitation of them, that we gain the power necessary for the kind of art we as moderns wish to create. . . . [f]or it is through art and art alone that peoples survive through the centuries. Their arts have been their most important historical records." (In his 1919 essay "Belly Music" Williams similarly demands "a new SIGHT of a SOURCE.")[19]

In exploring this strategy while staying in New Mexico, Hartley became interested in the *santos* alterpieces then common in the area. Barbara Haskell comments on this interest:

> By adopting his motifs directly from these painted or carved figures of saints, Hartley captured their primitive Christian mysticism. . . . Hartley's attraction to the simple religious expressiveness of the *santos* alterpieces paralleled his earlier fascination with Bavarian glass paintings and votive pictures. Equally appealing was the visual relationship between the primitive character of the *santos* and that in American folk art.[20]

Hartley's paintings are flat, two-dimensional designs that are often direct adaptations of Mexican-American altarpieces to his modernist mode. His 1921 poem "The Crucifixion of Noël" is a verbal expression of this interest. The poem synthesizes the Christmas and Easter stories; "Noël is crucified!!!" but "Noël is beautiful in his new position."[21]

Williams's work, beginning with the early "Homage" (1912) is often concerned with the focusing force of the icon figure. In "Homage" the female icon Elvira transforms her worshippers, uniting them as lovers. "March" limns Fra Angelico's *Annunciation* to tap its "energized past." But the strategy of contact insists that the saint motif be translated into contemporary terms. The modern icon, while partaking of the primitive mystical force of the old, must incorporate those "age conceptions" of which McAlmon saw Williams so "vividly aware." "A patron saint is one thing," Williams wrote in *Contact,* "but in the inter-communications of art there should be something more than conversations between men on the one hand and beasts on the other. . . . It is a common language we are seeking, a common language in which art itself is our St. Francis" (*SE,* 27, 29). Similarly, in writing to praise the editors of *The Little Review,* he told them, "You have your foot in the jam of the door and your services are flamingo-winged compared to those of the builders of the Cathedral of St. John the Divine."[22]

Williams's poem "St. Francis Einstein of the Daffodils" is an ambitious attempt to transform the saint motif into modern terms. The version in *Collected Earlier Poems* (*CEP,* 379) dates from 1936, and is a radically revised version of the poem that appeared in *Contact* in 1921.

Williams introduces the poem as in *Contact* a "sample poem" in a list of literary "commodities" which he offers for sale—the ironic humor reinforcing Hartley's contention of several months earlier that in America "the arts of painting and poetry . . . are the last to be bought and sold as valuable merchandise."[23]

Einstein arises "at the time in fashion," a Venus figure "out of the sea." He is spring incarnate, the "Savior of the daffodils," replacing that redundant idol "the dead Statue of Liberty," and also the "dead and buried" civilizations of Samos and Lesbos. He comes out of history:

> up from the sea
> in Thomas March Jefferson's
> black boat

but energized through his own "force of complicated mathematics." For Williams, Einstein's message of relativity lends scientific justification to the pattern of the new poem, the pattern that fuses poet and object into a new realm of imaginative co-existence.

> April Einstein . . .
> has come among the daffodils
> shouting
> that flowers and men
> were created
> relatively equal.
> Oldfashioned knowledge is
> dead under the blossoming peachtrees.

The poem calls attention to its status as patterned composition in the final six lines (cut from the revised version). They are a summary of the poem's central motifs, its inner logic—the logic behind the transformation of man to saint-figure to object to poem—Einstein become "It".

> It is Einstein
> out of complicated mathematics
> among the daffodils—
> spring winds blowing
> four ways, hot and cold,
> shaking the flowers![24]

On 4 May 1920 Hartley became secretary of Société Anonyme, Inc., a collective founded by Marcel Duchamp, Man Ray, and Katherine S. Dreir "to help clarify the mental atmosphere which befogs the modern paintings."[25] Hartley played an active role in the Société while he remained in New York. He lectured on 30 November 1920, took part in a symposium on 16 February 1921, and gave a talk—"What is Dadaism?"— appropriately on All-Fools Day of the same year. This latter talk appeared in his *Adventures in the Arts* as "The Importance of Being Dada" and received Williams's approval in *Spring and All* (*Imag,* 150).

Williams began to express an interest in Dada in the "Prologue" to *Kora in Hell*. Dada offered a possible strategy to accomplish that "purgation by thought"[26] he demanded of American poets and critics, a way to bring forth a pattern expressive of the contemporary moment. His 1919 poem "Complete Destruction" is a "purgation by thought" of the conventional structure and subject matter of a poem.

> It was an icy day,
> We buried the cat,
> then took her box
> and set match to it
>
> in the back yard.
> Those fleas that escaped
> earth and fire
> died by the cold.
>
> (*CEP,* 207)

(The image reappears in "St. Francis Einstein of the Daffodils": "Lesbia is / a black cat in the freshturned / garden.") But in these immediate postwar years Williams remained ambivalent about Dada, this "latest development of the French soul" as he called it. "America is a bastard country where decomposition is the prevalent spectacle but the contour is not particularly dadaesque and that's the gist of it." Dada, to have any relevance for American art, must be adapted to "local terms. As it is we should know what is before us, what it is and why. Or at least we should know our own part in the matter: which amounts to the same thing. Not that Dadaism is particularly important but—there it is" (*ARI,* 66).

But as Williams's praise of Hartley's Dada essay in *Spring and All* indicates, he soon became more interested in the possibilities of the movement. Its iconoclasm offered a strategy for American art to rid itself of European associations. By 1924, McAlmon, conducting him around Paris, could be dismayed that Williams "would have it" that the Dadaists "were profound and moved by a significant impetus."[27]

In view of Williams's close association with Hartley in the immediate postwar years, it is fitting that *Sour Grapes* concludes with a poem in homage to the painter. As noted earlier, Williams remembered *Sour Grapes* as a "mood book," reflecting "disappointment, sorrow" and isolation

(*IWWP,* 33, 34). But although "The Great Figure" (*CEP,* 230) has its own elements of irony and bitterness, it qualifies this mood in its assertion that poet and painter can together establish "contact." Working together, they can provide that "unity" which "alone can . . . afford dispersion of efforts" (*ARI,* 67).

This poem features in many discussions of Williams's interest in the visual arts, although critics usually look to a connection with Charles Demuth's famous poster portrait of the poet *I Saw the Figure 5 in Gold* (1928).[28] However the Hartley association, more than the connection with Demuth's later painting, reveals the full significance of "The Great Figure"—and the full significance of its position as the concluding poem of *Sour Grapes.*

This is how the poem appeared in that volume:

> Among the rain
> and lights
> I saw the figure 5
> in gold
> on a red
> firetruck
> moving
> with weight and urgency
> tense
> unheeded
> to gong clangs
> siren howls
> and wheels rumbling
> through the dark city.

In his autobiography Williams links the incident that produced the poem to a visit to Hartley's studio on Fifteenth Street, repeating the poem's association with Hartley in a 1956 interview with Emily Farnham.[29] (Hartley's correspondence narrows down the probable date of his visit—he lived at 337 W. 15th street in the second half of 1919, where McAlmon also rented a room.)

Williams writes in the *Autobiography*:

Once on a hot July day coming back exhausted from the Post Graduate Clinic, I dropped in as I sometimes did at Marsden's studio on Fifteenth Street for a talk, a little drink maybe and to see what he was doing. As I approached his number I heard a great clatter of bells and the roar of a fire engine passing the end of the street down Ninth Avenue. I turned just in time to see a golden figure 5 on a red background flash by. The impression was so sudden and forceful that I took a piece of paper out of my pocket and wrote a short poem about it.

Before continuing his account of the visit, Williams breaks his narrative to insert a later reminiscence. He recalls standing on a station platform with Hartley

> when an express train roared by right before our faces—crashing through making up time in a cloud of dust and sand so that we had to put up our hands to protect our faces.
>   As it passed Marsden turned and said to me, "That's what we all want to be, isn't it, Bill?" (*Auto,* 172)

The juxtaposition of the express train anecdote clearly associates the train, the speeding fire engine with its figure 5, and the painter Williams was about to visit. The connection is reinforced by the apparently casual reference that transforms Hartley and his studio into "his number." In an unpublished letter to Henry Wells in 1955 Williams pointed to this larger meaning, explaining, "In the case of *The Great Figure* I think you missed the irony of the word *great,* the contemptuous feeling I had at that moment for all 'frear figures' [*sic*] in public life compared with that figure 5 riding in state with full panoply down the streets of the city ignored by everyone but the artist."[30]

By alluding to his painter friend in terms of a numerical figure set against a dynamic, colorful background, Williams matched the strategy of Hartley's 1913–15 Berlin canvases. These abstract works, painted under the impact of his meeting with Kandinsky and Marc, fuse military, sexual,[31] and numerical symbols into what Hartley called "consultations of the eye . . . my notion of the purely pictorial."[32] As with Williams's figure 5, the numbers scattered across these canvases reflect not only the modernist aesthetic behind their composition, but also an esoteric quality peculiar to the scene or person abstractly portrayed. Many of the paintings gain further numerical associations through such abstractionist titles as *Painting No. 1, Painting No. 2,* etc. Most of the works, including *Painting No. 5* which Williams may have had specifically in mind, are dominated by the military colors of white, black, red, and gold, mirrored in "The Great Figure" by "lights," "dark," "red," and "gold."

Both Hartley and Williams emphasized their strategy of capturing the 'immediate.' Hartley insisted upon the spontaneity of his Berlin compositions, declaring, "The forms are only those which I have observed casually from day to day."[33] Williams similarly asserts that "The Great Figure" is the record of an "impression . . . sudden and forceful," despite the variant printed versions of his poem, and the manuscript evidence of their careful revision.[34]

Writing about Hartley five years after his friend's death in 1943, Williams singled out the Berlin pictures as the painter's most significant accomplishment. He could have seen the works at Stieglitz's 291 gallery in Spring, 1916 or January 1917, or at Hartley's studio, since many were unsold and remained in the painter's possession. Williams's sense of the dynamism, violence, and color of the paintings corresponds to the setting of "The Great Figure".

> Hartley knew Paris, and, more important, the Berlin of just before the First World War and painted there . . . abstract furies, close to the eye, pressing as it were on the eye, of great significance and beauty. . . . I have seen many attempts to equal them with their bold strokes of primary colors, exploding bombs, the arching trajectories of rockets. . . . It was a phenomenon unequalled in the history of art. If for nothing else these paintings of this period mark Marsden Hartley as one of the most powerful figures in American painting. (*ARI*, 153)

In the context of the Hartley association, "The Great Figure" achieves a level of meaning not noted by Williams's commentators. Rod Townley finds the poem's "tense / unheeded" to be "weak," while James Breslin claims of these lines that "Williams, uncertain that the object can speak for itself . . . speaks for it."[35] But the lines are in fact crucial, for like the figure, painter and poet are also "tense / unheeded." "The Great Figure" becomes a type of the artist isolated by an America inimical to its vital, creative talents. The painter still suffered poverty and neglect despite the "phenomenon" of his Berlin pictures, and Williams's work was still buried in little magazines and slim, self-financed volumes.

Yet the poet is about to visit the painter, and the poem finally affirms the hope that America's "unheeded" artists *can* support each other. As the final poem of *Sour Grapes,* "The Great Figure" qualifies the volume's "disappointment, sorrow." *Sour Grapes* fits into that pattern frequently structuring Williams's work: a despairing "descent," from which the poet emerges envisioning a rebirth of creative activity through the power of a rejuvenated imagination. But the hope that this poem's synthesis of poetry and painting represents—like the hope of "unity" that *Contact* represented—proved vain. In the summer of 1921 Hartley joined McAlmon and the other expatriates in Europe.

6

Spring and All

Williams's letters to Ezra Pound in the first half of the twenties reveal his considerable ambivalence about remaining in Rutherford while artist after artist packed his bags and left for Europe. Nevertheless, he determined to turn his isolation and local material to good account, publishing an extended prose harangue, *The Great American Novel,* in 1923, the prose and poems of *Spring and All* in the same year, and the historical essays of *In the American Grain* in 1925.

Williams's interest in the ideas and achievements of the visual artists continued to grow, and some of these interests were new. He began to feel that Dada was, after all, important. The painting and theories of Juan Gris excited him, and he discovered an important new friend in Charles Sheeler. Along with these new concerns, he continued to follow the work of Hartley and Demuth. All of these interests find a place in *Spring and All,* Williams's most complex and fully-realized expression of what he had learned from the painters.

Williams put aside his reservations about Dada in the early twenties. In the same year, 1920, that Williams declared his suspicions of "this French Orchid" in *Contact,* Pound and Hartley began to advocate the virtues of Dada. Now settled in Paris, Pound contributed to Tristan Tzara's *Dadaphone* and André Breton's *Littérature.* He met Picabia, and appeared in the painter's *391,* a Dadaist continuation of Stieglitz's *291.* Pound's earlier scorn (he had written to John Quinn in 1916 complaining of "all this modern froth . . . 291, Picabia, etc., etc., etc.,"[1]) changed to admiration. He praised the painter to Wyndham Lewis in 1921 "not exactly as a painter, but as a writer," although there is "more in his design stuff than comes up in reprod."[2] (Williams wrote to the editors of *The Little Review* in 1922 to praise their Picabia number.) Together Pound and Picabia took over *The Little Review* for a few issues, beginning with a Dada manifesto in the January/March 1921 number. Among the items Pound contributed were two nonsense pieces by "Abel Saunders" dedicated to "Bill Williams and Else von Johann Wolfgang Loringhoven y Fulano''—the items a response to the latter's Dadaesque review of *Kora in Hell* in an earlier issue.[3]

Pound and Williams differed radically from the European Dadaists in their continued insistence upon the fundamental value of art as a mode of expression. They wanted to retain a central role for art in articulating, and offering a solution for, the deepest social and cultural problems. Their interest in Dada was in its challenge to authority and conventions. For Williams, Dada suggested a way to break down those word patterns and word associations forged out of European experience, and now congealed into conventions that stifled the possibilities of a language and design expressive of the native American landscape and imagination.

As important to Williams as Pound's Dadaist exercises was Marsden Hartley's fleeting interest in the movement. Hartley's painting shows no evidence of this interest, which was more in the energy and iconoclasm of the Dadaists than anything else, but he appears alongside Duchamp and Man Ray in Richard Boix's drawing *New York Dada Group* (c. 1920). He contributed a piece, "Yours with Devotion; Trumpets and Drums," to the single appearance of *New York Dada* (1921), and on All-Fools Day the same year delivered his "What is Dada?" lecture to the Société Anonyme. In addition, he published some disjointed prose improvisations in *Contact*, and concluded his collection *Adventures in the Arts* with an essay titled "The Importance of Being 'Dada'."

On the final page of *Spring and All* Williams directs the reader interested in how the "imagination" can "free the world of fact from the imposition of 'art'" to "Hartley's last chapter" in *Adventures in the Arts* (*Imag*, 150). Many of Hartley's themes appear in *Spring and All*. Foremost among these is Hartley's dismissal of the cyclical theories of art history that had provided the intellectual basis for expressionism and that are the background to such *Al Que Quiere*! poems as "January Morning," "History" and "March." Hartley announces, "I turn from my place in the scheme from expressionist to dada-ist." This frees him to undertake contemporary, native expression: "Art is then a matter of how one is to take life now, and not by any means a matter of how the Greeks or Egyptians or any other race has shown it to be for their own needs and satisfaction. If art was necessary to them, it is unnecessary to us now, therefore it is free to express itself as it will."[4] Similarly, in *The Great American Novel* Williams now finds the American writer thwarted by "pyramids, pyramids of words, tombs" (*Imag*, 160), whereas "pyramids" and "tombs" were key symbols of the "energized past" in "History," "March" and "Overture to a Dance of Locomotives."

Williams insists that the patterns of *Spring and All* are attuned to an

American moment born out of a universal, not merely a European, history. The typographical chaos and syntactic confusion of the opening prose pages break down cultural and historical continuity, preparing the way for a new world of imaginative potential. In the opening poem this potential is dramatized by a scene that conflates the personal history of the poet (this is his route to work), and the history of the landscape and continent, through language that discriminates carefully between the particular of the moment and the imaginative continuity of its context.

> They enter the new world naked,
> cold, uncertain of all
> save that they enter. All about them
> the cold, familiar wind—
>
> (*Imag*, 95)

"They" here are simultaneously the poet's perceptions, the first growths of spring, the poem's newly minted words, and the first entrance of the pioneers onto the soil of "the new world." Within *Spring and All*'s own history of the imagination, these early European spectators absorb the new landscape around them, holding in abeyance the linguistic and perceptual conventions shaped by the continent they have left behind. Concurrently, Williams was describing in his *In the American Grain* the *actual* settlers' failure to respond to the potential of their new landscape.

Hartley argues in "What is Dada?" that Dada's acerbic approach produces "the utter annihilation of sentimentality, of legend, of what we call poetry." This approach opens the way for the emergence of "a larger, newer variety of matter, more relevant to our especial need, our modernity." The destruction of archaic forms leads to the perception and use of new material, new patterns, to be expressed through "the most spontaneous and consequently the least logical lyricism." "I ride my own hobbyhorse away from the dangers of art which is with us a modern vice at present into the wide expanse of magnanimous diversion from which I may extract all the joyousness I am capable of, from the patterns I encounter."[5]

In Poem VIII of *Spring and All* we find a "spontaneous . . . lyricism" contrasted with the "modern vice" of art. The financier J. Pierpont Morgan serves as a symbol of the American patron directing his interests and money to artists long dead, to art that has no relevance to contemporary, native expression. The poem's opening four stanzas demonstrate a "spontaneous . . . lyricism" that can conjoin the patterns of sunlight through a window with the language of technology. This lyrical expression can also incorporate Persephone, Williams's goddess of the imagination.

The sunlight in a
yellow plaque upon the
varnished floor

is full of a song
inflated to
fifty pounds pressure

at the faucet of
June that rings
the triangle of the air

pulling at the
anemones in
Persephone's cow pasture—

J. P. M then "leaps" from a landscape usurped by commercial concerns.

When from among
the steel rocks leaps
J. P. M.

The imaginative possibilities represented by Persephone/Kora/"core" are repressed through a design sense that limits itself to industrial manufactures, and a narrow and commercial approach to art.

who enjoyed
extraordinary privileges
among virginity

to solve the core
of whirling flywheels
by cutting

the Gordian knot
with a Veronese or
perhaps a Rubens—

Morgan's legacy is to kill the "spontaneous . . . lyricism" that can pattern the modern particulars of light and landscape. The financier's son, also "J. P. M.," had inherited his father's financial empire in 1913, and had continued his father's practice of purchasing European masters.

And so it comes
to motor cars—
which is the son

leaving off the g
of sunlight and grass—

Nevertheless, the poem absorbs this part of America's industrial history into its own pattern, the pattern being a full response to modern conditions. The poem concludes as it opens, with a display of the materials and potential relationships available to a poem that will release, not try to "solve," the "core" of imagination:

Impossible

to say, impossible
to underestimate—
wind, earthquakes in

Manchuria, a
partridge
from dry leaves
(Imag, 109–10)

Morgan's son also appears in "Rome," a collection of improvisational pieces that Williams composed on his 1924 European trip, and immediately after his return to Rutherford. Williams inserts into a series of improvisations on "the value of new" [*sic*] a letter from the financier to the *New York Times.* Morgan's letter stresses the need for investor security with regard to German bonds. His opening sentence, an assertion of routine, is the antithesis of Williams's demand for the "new": "I am sailing for my annual holiday, in accordance with plans made months ago." Williams subsequently notes the "similarity between" Morgan's letter and a noted medical lecturer's "explanation of liver degeneration," where "from an impoverished blood, the outer part gets all the nourishment and the center degenerates."[6]

Williams's interest in Dada led him to a close association with Harold Loeb's new magazine *Broom* (through his friendship with one of its editors, Maxwell Josephson, he met Charles Sheeler). *Broom,* started in 1921, was initially anti-Dada, espousing the line of *The Seven Arts* and of Waldo Frank's *Our America,* that artists should celebrate those spiritual values that are necessary to offset the losses caused by dehumanizing technology. But Loeb soon became interested in the iconoclasm of Dada, and shifted *Broom*'s position. After the fourth issue Alfred Kreymborg resigned in protest, and Josephson—"mad on Dadaism since being in Paris" Burke told Williams—joined the magazine.[7]

Secession, founded at the same time by Gorham Munson, took the opposite route. While its first issues gave a good deal of space to Dada concerns, it subsequently began to defend Frank and Rosenfeld's call for an order to offset the anarchy of Dada. Despite Kenneth Burke's association with *Secession,* Williams's sympathies were with *Broom. Secession* only carried two of Williams's poems, while *Broom* published many of his pieces, including a number of the *In the American Grain* essays.[8]

One of the particulars that characterized modern life for the American Dadaists—American life especially—was the growth of industry, and they insisted that American art take account of this. It was here that *Broom* and *Secession* differed once *Secession* began to embrace Frank's antitechnological views. Fittingly, *Broom* ran a warm tribute to Robert Coady upon his death in 1921. In his *The Soil* Coady had early insisted upon the central place of American industrial technology in native expression.

Poem VIII of *Spring and All* contrasts the imaginative incorporation of industry into a poem with that narrow commercialism of "J. P. M.'"s that would subjugate art to market forces. Poem XXV is an even more direct engagement with the forces of modern technology. The first lines of the poem address the apparent antagonism between poetry and the modern world it would incorporate.

> Somebody dies every four minutes
> in New York State—
>
> To hell with you and your poetry—
> You will rot and be blown
> through the next solar system
> with the rest of the gases—
>
> What the hell do you know about it?

The admonitory "AXIOMS" that follow resolve this antagonism.

> AXIOMS
>
> Do not get killed
>
> Careful Crossing Campaign
> Cross Crossings Cautiously

These "AXIOMS" are functional particulars of the modern world, apparently slogans from a safety-campaign poster, and they display a concise, purposeful linguistic response to the modern facts of high speed and the motor car. The poem absorbs these linguistic particulars into its own compositional pattern, resolving the specious antagonism. Art can conquer death and time by being alive to the contour of its time. Ironically, the poem absorbs this particular of modern life by *ignoring* its cautionary message. In being alive to his time the poet chooses the risk of inclusion before the safety of echoing conventional pattern. By recklessly allowing the language of sidewalk signs to "cross" into the poem, Williams allows their alliterative admonitions to "cross" into the world of the imagination.

The poem subsequently absorbs the exhortations of what reads like a subway poster—the poster and the poem's conciseness of language united in a plea for Americans to investigate their own landscape.

Outings in New York City

Ho for the open country

Don't stay shut up in hot rooms
Go to one of the Great Parks
Pelham Bay for example

It's on Long Island Sound
with bathing, boating
tennis, baseball, golf, etc.

Acres and acres of green grass
wonderful shade trees, rippling brooks

Take the Pelham Bay Park Branch
of the Lexington Ave. (East Side)
Line and you are there in a few
minutes

Interborough Rapid Transit Co.
(*Imag*, 146–47)

In poem XXV poetry is made out of objects, signs and posters, paralleling Coady's and Duchamp's insistence that the products of modern technology were themselves art. One of the examples in this poem, billposters, was the subject of an essay by Josephson in *Broom,* titled "The Great American Billposter." It was a common theme of the modernist writers that advertising slogans displayed far more of the necessary virtues of economy, and of response to modern concerns, than the writings of conventional poets. Josephson's contribution is a reply to a symposium of "Thirty Americans (intellectuals)" who had called for the abolition of the billposter. For Josephson, this is another insidious attempt to import "approved European methods of living or painting or writing." Billposters, he asserts, are "the 'folklore' of modern times," part of the "effervescent revolving cacophonous milieu" that modern art must take account of. Josephson's other examples of this "milieu" are all to be found in *Spring and All,* for they form the set of motifs which the American Dadaists felt most characterized the contemporary environment: "the Cinema transports us, the newspapers intone their gaudy jargon . . . athletes play upon the frenetic passions of baseball crowds, and skyscrapers rise lyrically to the exotic rhythms of jazz bands which upon waking up we find to be nothing but the drilling of pneumatic hammers on steel girders."[9]

When Williams arrived in Paris in 1924 he was eager to meet the French Dadaists. McAlmon recalled, "Bill was intent on meeting young French writers, the Dadaists, Tristan Tzara . . . to get to the root of what they were driving at."[10] But by 1924 the Dada movement was burning itself out, and André Breton was formulating the dicta of surrealism— combining Dada's qualities of the absurd and fantastic with an interest in the subconscious. Pound was never to take an interest in the later movement, and Williams not for some years.

In Williams's 1924 improvisations that make up his "Rome" manuscript, he finally puts Dada aside. The Dadaists' response to the local and the moment had remained local and momentary; "The modernist is he who sees through the modern—to an essential and continuous organization that exists in it."[11] This continuity, symbolized so often in Williams's work by the figure of Kora, is the source of the primeval imaginative power that he set against Eliot's notion of "tradition." It is the "discoverable value which is the antithesis of arrangements, traditions which are the accidents of its occurrence, the lime, the pulp—and have nothing at all to do with it." This was the truth that "the Dada's felt, DIMLY, weakly. They skirted the edge but without seeing it CLEARLY."[12]

For Williams, the Dadaists lacked a sense of that vital context that makes "destruction and creation . . . simultaneous." And this is also his criticism of Duchamp's abandonment of art. Duchamp was in New York through much of 1922 and the early months of 1923. When he left for Europe that year, he announced his abandonment of the Large Glass, *The Bride Stripped Bare by Her Bachelors, Even,* that he had been working on for eight years. Duchamp's concerns in constructing the glass had paralleled many of Williams's own—the resolution of male and female energies, the interrelationship of complex patterns, the emphasis upon an internal compositional rationale, and the transformation of glass from a "barrier" to a part of the composition itself. Williams insisted in *Contact* that the implications of Duchamp's renunciation were limited to the Frenchman's own development as an artist.

> We say only in view of Marcel's intelligent and devastating silence . . . there is no comment on pictures but pictures, on music but music, poems but poetry. . . . Combinations of glass are combinations of glass, without value as a critique of pigments mixed with oil and spread upon cloth . . . there is no excuse in these things for BAD WRITING.
> Nor does work in glass, wire, sun-prints, etc., abolish the use of other modes.

> The only thing that the occasional work of such a man as Marcel ABOLISHES is bad work in every line of endeavor—BAD WRITING.[13]

Williams finally rejects Duchamp and the Dadaists because they fail to acknowledge that crucial context he felt as an essential counterpoint to modernist iconoclasm, the "essential and continuous organization" that the patterned works of Gris, Demuth and Sheeler always recognized. The postscript to Williams's Dada interests is his brief contribution to the final American Dada effort, *Aesthete 1925,* in which he questions the usefulness of the whole exercise.[14]

In his autobiography Williams lists "Juan Gris—at one time my favorite painter" among the modernist pioneers now "dead," (*Auto,* 318). Gris's painting and writing held a central position in Williams's thinking during the twenties and early thirties. Gris is not mentioned in his writings before *Spring and All,* although Williams had had opportunities to see his work. The Coady Gallery in Washington Square had displayed some works in 1916, and reproductions had appeared in *The Soil.* In addition, the Arensbergs owned five works. But it was not until the early 1920s that Gris's work began to appear frequently in the little magazines. *The Little Review* devoted a complete issue to the painter in 1924. Loeb was a strong admirer of his work, often publishing reproductions in *Broom,* and writing an appreciative essay for the August 1923 issue.

Williams met Loeb in New York in 1923, and to judge from a letter Loeb wrote Williams at this time the two were in agreement over painters and painting.

> I have always wished to know you. . . . My expectations were more than realized during our two enjoyable evenings for I found out that not only did we look at literature from much the same angle but that you are the only resident of America that reacted to the reproductions in Broom according to their value. Most everyone else liked the worst pictures best and the best not at all.[15]

Demuth probably also contributed to Williams's notice of Gris. He had been an admirer of his work since meeting the painter in 1914, and as his own style moved towards precisionism, he would have found Gris's brand of synthetic cubism, retaining the recognizability of the motif, especially appealing. Demuth visited Europe for three months in 1921, being forced to return prematurely because of illness, but during his brief visit he wrote to Stieglitz singling out two magazines as of especial interest—*L'Espirit Nouveau* and *L'Amour D'Art.*[16] Both magazines gave a good deal of attention to Gris. *L'Espirit Nouveau* was established to propagate the ideas of Le Corbusier and Amédée Ozenfant first set out in their 1918 manifesto *Après le Cubisme.* They attacked the decorative tendencies of cubism, demanding an art "as pure and 'rigorous' as the machine . . . general, static, expressing the constant factor in nature" while exhibiting "clarity, precision, fidelity to the 'concept.'"[17] This doctrine of "purism" had a strong influence in the early twenties, particularly upon Demuth and Charles Sheeler. Williams was interested enough to own a copy of Ozenfant's *La peinture moderne*.[18]

In its fifth issue *L'Espirit Nouveau* carried a long article by Maurice Raynal on Gris, together with thirteen reproductions of Gris's work. Raynal set out Gris's aesthetic, and the painter added a foreword giving his approval.[19] Gris spelled out the same aesthetic himself in "Notes on my Painting" in the summer of 1923, and the following year in "On the Possibilities of Painting," originally a Sorbonne lecture. (The essays appeared in *Der Querschnitt* and *The Transatlantic Review,* both magazines that also printed Williams's work).[20]

Williams thought highly of Gris's essays, and when he wrote to Kay Boyle in 1932 calling for a "form" that "will take its shape from the character of its age," he added, "Why do we not read more of Juan Gris? He knew these things in painting and wrote well of them" (*SL,* 130). Gris emphasized that his art was one of synthesis, and that the resultant composition reflected "the period. Every aesthetic should bear a date . . . no important work of art can belong to any period but its own, to the very moment of its creation." His aesthetic insisted upon the autonomy of the finished composition, and the composition's roots in clearly seen and felt particulars. The artist searched the object, Gris argued, for that "basic idea" that lay beyond its utilitarian functions and symbolic associations. The artist's perception of this "basic idea" was directed by "an emotion" within him characteristic of "the aesthetic outlook of the period." The artist's composition synthesized "these elements", that usually pass unrealized. The spectator, returning from the picture back to the world of objects, found his perception directed by the composition's synthesis. Thus, Gris claimed, the artist can "make subject 'x' coincide with the picture that [he] has in mind," rather "than to make picture 'x' co-incide with a given subject."[21] Williams's recapitulation in his "A Novelette" of 1930 is: "I have always admired and partaken of Juan Gris. Singly he says that the actual is the drawing of the face—and so the face borrowing of the drawing—by lack of copying and lack of a burden to the story— is real" (*Imag,* 286). Discussing Gris's *The Open Window* (1921) in *Spring and All* Williams observes: "The attempt is being made to separate things of the imagination from life. . . . Here is a shutter, a bunch of grapes, a sheet of music, a picture of sea and mountains (particularly fine) which the onlooker is not for a moment permitted to witness as an 'illusion'" (*Imag,* 110).

The modernist painters all emphasized that the imaginative artifact was separate from "life," drawing its status and compositional integrity from its existence as an artifact. But Gris (and Demuth and Sheeler) retained the recognizability of the object, while still making no concessions to the conventions of realism. Since Williams, along with many of the American avant-garde, was calling for American art to concern itself with native material, the recognizability of the object was important. To the "onlooker", Williams argued, Gris's art offered "things with which he is familiar, simple things—at the same time to detach them from ordinary experience to the imagination" (*Imag*, 110).

Williams demanded of the poem what Gris demanded of painting. In *Spring and All* he insists, "Poetry has to do with the crystallization of the imagination—the perfection of new forms as additions to nature" (*Imag*, 140), and later, "Poetry liberates the words from their emotional implications" (*Imag*, 145). The poet controls the compositional contour of his poem, sensitive to, and realizing, the potential of his medium as an imaginative pattern. Thus Marianne Moore's "words remain separate, each unwilling to group with the others except as they move in the one direction" (*Imag*, 146). Williams describes Gris's *The Open Window* as the control of patterned direction, "One thing laps over on the other, the cloud laps over on the shutter, the bunch of grapes is part of the handle of the guitar," and also the control of interpretation, "The mountain and sea are obviously not 'the mountain and sea,' but a picture of the mountain and the sea" (*Imag*, 110–11); they become "things" in themselves, in and through the painting.

Poem IX of *Spring and All*, which follows this discussion of Gris, is an exercise in liberating "words [and subject] from their emotional implications." The poem first questions the purpose of the preceding prose arguments, and then recalls a spring affair "fifteen years ago" with "Miss Margaret Jarvis" at "the hospital."[22]

What about all this writing?

O "Kiki"
O Miss Margaret Jarvis
The backhandspring

I:clean
    clean
    clean: yes . . . New-York

Wrigley's, appendicitis, John Marin:
skyscraper soup—

Either that or a bullet!

It is helpful in reading these lines to recall the prose discussion that immediately precedes the discussion of Gris. The subject is the same—the nature of the imaginative act, and its relationship to external things. The discussion is leading up to "the feeling of completion" that Gris's work gives, but Williams first explores other possible ways to obtain "completion."

> Even the most robust constitution has its limits, though the Roman feast with its reliance upon regurgitation to prolong it shows an active ingenuity, yet the powers of a man are so pitifully small, with the ocean to swallow—that at the end of the feast nothing would be left but suicide.
>
> That or the imagination which in this case takes the form of humor, is known in that form—the release from physical necessity. Having eaten to the full we must acknowledge our insufficiency since we have not annihilated all food nor even the quantity of a good sized steer. (*Imag,* 106)

These sterile strategies for obtaining "completion" are echoed in the opening lines of Poem IX—its references to chewing gum, stomachache, and the "soup"-like expressionism of John Marin ("not a draughtsman," Williams told Emily Farnham; "I could never see Marin as an artist. Surely drawing is a basic thing in painting?").[23] "Suicide" is another possibility in the prose discussion, "Either that or a bullet!" in the poem.

The alternative to regurgitation or annihilation is to delve beneath "emotional implications." Paralleling Gris's insistence upon discovering the "basic idea," Williams argues, "Truly men feel an enlargement before great or good work, an expansion but this is not, as so many believe today a 'lie,' a stupefaction, a kind of mesmerism, a thing to block out 'life,' bitter to the individual, by a 'vision of beauty.' It is a work of the imagination. It gives the feeling of completion by revealing the oneness of experience" (*Imag,* 107). After discussing Gris's achievement of completion, Williams acknowledges that the modern stress upon the unifying compositional imperatives "was not necessary when the subject of art was not 'reality' but related to the 'gods'—by force, or otherwise," i.e. already imaginative (*Imag,* 111).

Poem IX continues with another false strategy, a romantic indulgence that, in the concluding lines, turns Margaret Jarvis into a saint-figure.

> Once
> anything might have happened
> You lay relaxed on my knees—
> the starry night
> spread out warm and blind
> above the hospital—

. . . .
but I merely
caress you curiously

fifteen years ago and you still
go about the city, they say
patching up sick school children

But the passion of the poet's engagement with the girl is released
only when he is most dispassionate:

Pah!

It is unclean
which is not straight to the mark—

In my life the furniture eats me

the chairs, the floor
the walls
which heard your sobs
drank up my emotion—
they which alone know everything

and snitched on us in the morning—

What to want?
Drunk we go forward surely
Not I

beds, beds, beds
elevators, fruit, night-tables
breasts to see, white and blue—
to hold in the hand, to nozzle

It is not onion soup
Your sobs soaked through the walls
breaking the hospital to pieces

Everything
—windows, chairs
obscenely drunk, spinning—
white, blue, orange
—hot with our passion

wild tears, desperate rejoinders
my legs, turning slowly
end over end in the air!

The series of images that displace the romantic nostalgia are the poem's
imposition of its own order over the patterns of nostalgic recall of the

actual event. This compositional order is built out of the perceptual discoveries that come from dispassionately realizing discrete particulars.

> But what would you have?
>
> All I said was:
> there, you see, it is broken
>
> stockings, shoes, hairpins
> your bed, I wrapped myself round you—
>
> I watched.
>
> You sobbed, you beat your pillow
> you tore your hair
> you dug your nails into your sides
>
> I was your nightgown
>   watched!
>   *(Imag, 113–15)*

The force of imagination that stresses the separation of modern art from
"life" (necessary because modern art is not obviously "related to the
'gods'") is isolated and isolating. *Spring and All* itself is addressed not
to a reader but "to the imagination" (*Imag,* 89). In the prose before
poem IX Williams writes, "Surely in isolation one becomes a god?—At
least one becomes something of everything, which is not wholly god-like,
yet a little so—in many things" (*Imag,* 111–12). Gris observed similarly,
"It is . . . by being my own spectator that I extract the subject from my
picture."[24]

    This isolating imagination controls the way the central section of the
poem presents the fifteen-year-old memory, and the reader is obliged to
follow the enforced direction, although it cuts against the nostalgic or
narrative pattern that his own sympathies might want to impose; "The
onlooker is not for a moment permitted to witness . . . an illusion."

    Poem VI insists upon its status as an imaginative word-pattern. What
would appear to be a personal declaration, "nothing that I have done,"
is immediately dissected as a grammatical construction. The poet is sub-
sumed into the letters of his poem—"I" becoming "the diphthong/ae."

> No that is not it
> nothing that I have done
> nothing
> I have done
>
> is made up of
> nothing
> and the diphthong

ae

together with
the first person
singular
indicative

of the auxiliary
verb
to have

. . . .
everything
I have done
is the same

if to do

is capable
of an
infinity of
combinations

involving the
moral
physical
and religious

codes

for everything
and nothing
are synonymous
when

energy in vacuo
has the power
of confusion

which only to
have done nothing
can make
perfect
                    (*Imag,* 103–5)

The poem contains the potential for an "infinity of combinations"—the potential caught in the infinitive "to do"—if it is allowed to be a pattern of words, "energy in vacuo," unconstrained by the burden of imposed conventions. The poem needs "nothing" to make it "perfect"; its "perfect" tense is its final stamp of self-sufficiency.

But viewing Poem VI alongside Poem V, which immediately precedes it, offers a further perspective. In its existence as a self-referential word-construction Poem VI contrasts with the poet's earlier work—"How easy to slip / into the old mode, how hard to / cling firmly to the advance—'' (Poem V). "Everything / I have done / is the same" as the analyzed word-pattern "nothing / I have done" only "if" the poet's earlier work separates words from "life" as Poem VI does. But the equation finally rests upon potential, the "capability" of the infinitive "to do" rather than the achievement of "an / infinity of / combinations." "Everything / and nothing / are synonymous" only if the poet had "done nothing."

In *Spring and All* Williams often makes the modern artist's newfound control of his material part of a poem's theme and structure, disrupting the expected stanzaic patterns and word groupings, or, as in Poem IX, the expected 'poetic' treatment of an emotional theme. As this chapter will demonstrate, the control of pattern finally extends to the overall structure of *Spring and All* itself.

In Poem XIII the stanzas 'overlap,' much like the objects in *The Open Window,* denying any reading that would impose a preconceived pattern upon them.

> Crustaceous
> wedge
> of sweaty kitchens
> on rock
> overtopping
> thrusts of the sea
>
> Waves of steel
> from
> swarming backstreets
> shell
> of coral
> inventing
> electricity—
>
> Lights
> speckle
> El Greco
> lakes
> in renaissance
> twilight
> with triphammers
>
> which pulverize
> nitrogen
> of old pastures
> to dodge
> motorcars
> with arms and legs—

```
        The aggregate
        is untamed
        encapsulating
        irritants
        but
        of agonized spires
        knits
        peace
            (Imag, 124–25)
```

The poem is here that "aggregate" which encapsulates the "irritants"—
the words and particulars. Both "irritants" and "aggregate" are "untamed," and both are also "encapsulating"; the syntax moves in both directions. The poem encapsulates the words, and the words encapsulate
the integrity of the observed particular, neither allowing semantic, syntactic, or stanzaic conventions to 'tame' their pattern. The stanzas are
"knitted" through this multiple direction, and through the overlapping of
"sea / Waves," "electricity—/ Lights," and "triphammers / which pul-
verize." The image of "agonized spires" recalls Williams's argument that
art "related to the 'gods,'" was imaginative by definition, not attempting
to mirror conventions of perception through conventions of form. Religious themes are now as restrictive and limited as all other rules and
conventions, but through incorporating the displaced imaginative quality
that the art of "the 'gods'" represents, the poem "knits / peace" out of
its multiple directions and "untamed / encapsulating / irritants—" "knits"
the perfect word for the multiple links of this poem.

The image of "agonized spires" may also be a glance at Demuth's
paintings of New England and Pennsylvania churches. These works are
centered upon the geometrical analysis, from multiple perspectives, of a
church spire, the convoluted, broken lines of the spire "knitting" the
surrounding ray lines into the painting's network of linear patterns. (There
may be a further homage to Demuth in the poem's reference to El Greco,
one of Demuth's favorite painters. One of his 1919 works is entitled *A
Sky After El Greco.*)

Gris's ability to present "familiar, simple things" that "are seen to
be in some peculiar way detached" is also a quality Williams admired in
the painter's early supporter Gertrude Stein. In his article "French Painting," written two or three years after *Spring and All,* Williams spelled
out her strategy to release the word from hackneyed associations, and he
specifically linked her approach to that of the painters: "The writer is to
describe, to represent just as the painter must do—but what? and how?
It is the same question of words and technique in their arrangement—
Stein has stressed, as Braque did paint, words" (*EK,* 22–23).

In *Spring and All* Williams calls for "the word" to be freed "from the fixities which destroy it" (*Imag,* 150). This freedom is the theme of Poem VII (it is actually unnumbered), later titled "The Rose." The poem possibly pays homage to both Gris and Stein. While it punctuates the prose discussion of Gris's *The Open Window,* the hackneyed word that the poem liberates is "rose"—an example that Stein had made her own. The poem may particularly allude to Gris's 1914 collage *Fleurs,* owned by Stein, and later titled *Roses.*

Some commentators have suggested that the prose immediately preceding the poem refers to Gris's *Fleurs;* "But such a picture as that of Juan Gris, though I have not seen it in color, is important as marking more clearly than any I have seen what the modern trend is" (*Imag,* 107). But when this passage is seen alongside the continuation of the discussion after Poems VII and VIII (*Imag,* 110) it is clear that Williams is referring to *The Open Window.*[25] While *The Open Window* appeared in *Broom*'s January 1922 issue (in black and white), *Fleurs* was not reproduced until 1928, in *Cahiers D'Art*[26] Williams may have seen a reproduction when visiting Harold Loeb, for Loeb frequently published Gris's work in *Broom.* Alternatively, Demuth or Hartley, both frequent visitors to Stein at 27 Rue de Fleures at one time, may have seen the collage and remarked on it to Williams. That Stein frequently spoke of Gris to her visitors is evident in the unfriendly report of the American artist George Biddle. "Nothing seemed very comfortable and there were some Picassos and a good many Juan Gris' hanging around. . . . She said something about Juan Gris being one of the great unrecognized creative spirits of his epoch."[27]

Writing of Gris in his 1930 "A Novelette," Williams noted "always the one thing in Juan Gris. Conversation as design" (*Imag,* 286). Similarly in "French Painting" he remarked of Stein, her "personal motto—A rose is a rose—. . . printed in a circle means two things." The first meaning is denotational. But the second emphasizes words as elements of form under the artist's control: "words which stand for all words and are very definitely not roses—but are nevertheless subject to arrangement for effect" (*EK,* 22–23). Poem VII begins, "The rose is obsolete," and two subsequent lines make clear that what is obsolete are the stale emotional associations of the word as symbol: "The rose carried weight of love / but love is at an end—of roses."

But "the end" is not only the exhaustion of romantic symbolism, it is also "the edge," the beginning of word and object seen anew, renewed with the potential to take its place with other words, other objects, as part of a compositional pattern.

But if it ends
the start is begun
so that to engage roses
becomes a geometry—

Sharper, neater, more cutting
figured in majolica—
the broken plate
glazed with a rose

Somewhere the sense
makes copper roses
steel roses—

The rose carried weight of love
but love is at an end—of roses

It is at the edge of the
petal that love waits

Freed from emotional "fixities," both words and object are capable of "arrangement" by the imagination "for effect". The poem throws up questions regarding direction now that the conventional patterns have been broken: "whither? . . . / what." But compositional pattern is not preconceived; it emerges out of the development of the composition. Gris insisted, "I never know in advance the appearance of the object represented. . . . It is the appearance of the work as a whole which is its culmination, for this aspect is unknown to me."[28] And it was in these terms that Williams wrote of Stein in 1930:

> Writing, like everything else, is much a question of refreshed interest. It is directed, not idly, but as most often happens (though not necessarily so) toward that point not to be predetermined where movement is blocked (by the end of logic perhaps). It is about these parts, if I am not mistaken, that Gertrude Stein will be found. (*Imag*, 351)

Thus the renewed energies of "the rose" allow object and word unlimited design potential—as in Stein's circular printing of her famous phrase "a rose is a rose is a rose," Gris's multiplication of the shape in the cut-outs of his collage *Fleurs,* and the cutting edge of the revitalized word, unconstrained, in the final image of Poem VII.

The place between the petal's
edge and the

From the petal's edge a line starts
that being of steel
infinitely fine, infinitely

rigid penetrates
the Milky Way
without contact—lifting
from it—neither hanging
nor pushing—

The fragility of the flower
unbruised
penetrates spaces
                (*Imag*, 107–9)

Along with Williams's interest in the European aesthetics of Dada and Gris went his continued insistence that the American artist use local material. The writers and artists closely associated with Alfred Stieglitz— Waldo Frank, Paul Rosenfeld, John Marin, and Georgia O'Keefe—also stressed the importance for American art of local "sensual . . . contacts." Williams drew closer to the group in the early twenties, although he always remained disturbed by the vatic tone of their writings. His keenest interest among American artists continued to lie with his friend Demuth, and also with his new acquaintance, Sheeler. The precisionist strategy of these two painters matched Williams's demand that the closely observed particular be transformed into the universal significance of imaginative composition, while the composition remained recognizable as utilizing local "sensual . . . contacts."

As noted earlier in this study, commentators have differed in their assessment of Williams's debt to, and interest in, the Stieglitz group. Williams himself is inconsistent, praising Stieglitz's pioneering use of American subject matter in "The American Background: America and Alfred Stieglitz," scorning the man in "What of Alfred Stieglitz?" (*ARI*, 177–79) and barely mentioning him in his autobiography. Williams was not published in the Stieglitz-influenced *Seven Arts*, but he was in its short-lived postwar successor *Manuscripts*. Nevertheless, he was never a "follower" in any sense. After all, it was Kreymborg, not Williams, who severed links with *Broom* after Loeb's criticism of Rosenfeld. And it was to Kreymborg that Rosenfeld turned, in 1934, for an account of Stieglitz's relationship with the writers. Sherwood Anderson, close to the group in these years, listed many of the people he had known in notes for his *Memoirs*—included are Waldo Frank, Hartley, Kreymborg, Marin, Rosenfeld and Stieglitz—but not Williams.[29] However, Williams was an eclectic thinker, taking from groups and individual artists what met his concerns of the moment. Whatever his misgivings about some of the group's work, he embraced their emphasis upon the sensual and the local.

Rosenfeld's article "American Painting" appeared in *The Dial* of December 1921, and was later revised for his *The Port of New York*. His argument is similar to Williams's in *In The American Grain* (begun in 1922) that American artists have habitually avoided utilizing in their art the new landscape that confronted them. Rosenfeld argues that the first steps towards native expression in American painting occur with the work of Albert Ryder.

> Slowly, painfully, the minds began to turn towards self-expression, towards acceptance of self, of the vague and menacing American future. The new rhythm had been consented in. Of that first, difficult, steep, contact with local conditions, contact with what for want of a closer term one calls "the soil," the art of Ryder is the breath, the suspiration.[30]

This is the same historical pattern of fear, and a belated, promising response, that Williams maps out in *Spring and All* and *In the American Grain*. When he contributed the essay "The American Background" to the *America and Alfred Stieglitz* volume in 1934, he continued the approach. The history he tells is of the American people's slow "adjustment to the conditions around them" (*SE,* 141). Williams praises Stieglitz in this essay for having the courage to respond to the local environment, his camera attending to "the immediate and the actual" as he selectively incorporated European strategies into the expression of the America he saw teeming around him (*SE,* 160).

Williams did not subscribe to Rosenfeld's ranking of the most significant native artists in "American Painting," and this is in large part because of his different conception of how the native "particular" was to be expressed. Williams's emphasis upon "edge" and pattern stressed a disciplined austerity of line in poetry and painting. The process of revitalizing the perceived particular and transforming it into a compositional element consisted in paring down superfluous language and "decorative" visual detail in order to capture the essence, and to see "through the modern—to an essential and continuous organization that exists in it." This was the strategy behind Gris's demand for the "basic idea." But for Rosenfeld, as for many of the Stieglitz group, the significance of the realized particular was a spiritual one. The artist was first perceiver, and then prophet. As far as Williams was concerned, this was to weigh down the particular—object, word, or compositional element—with matter just as extraneous as the conventional associations that had been discarded. Rosenfeld demanded full uninhibited expression of the "spirit" of the American object. Using this measure, he finds Demuth and Hartley pusillanimous, but has unreserved praise for Stieglitz, Marin, O'Keefe, and Arthur Dove. These artists bring "the entire man, dream interpenetrated with reality, and reality with dream, to the composition of their works."[31]

According to the French critic in Williams's *The Great American Novel,* Williams's idea of expressing his American background is to "have no notion what you are going to write from one word to the other. It is madness" (*Imag,* 196). Rejecting the critic's call for a lyrical strain in the style of Anderson or Masters, Williams's strategy is the pell-mell prose of *Spring and All,* and the disjointed syntax of the poems. Rosenfeld complains of "unfulfillment" in American painting, but Williams insists that a fully realized response to local conditions includes notice of the factors hostile to full expression. Rosenfeld finds in the "slightly chilling beauty" of Hartley's "frozen art" evidence of the painter's "starvation and imprisonment, vain writings and death in life."[32] But in contrast, this is Williams's praise of Poe's response to local conditions, from *In the American Grain:* "He sought by stress upon construction to hold the loose-strung mass off *even at the cost of an icy coldness of appearance*; it was the first need of his time, an escape from the formless mass he hated." In Poe's work "the grotesque inappropriateness of the life about him forced itself in among his words" (*IAG,* 221, 220; my emphasis).

This dilemma matches that facing the central character of *Paterson,* for Williams clearly regards Poe's "local conditions" as similar in many ways to his own. The fragmentary surface texture of *In the American Grain, Spring and All,* and *Paterson* (and of Williams's individual poems)— juxtaposition of disparate elements, convoluted or disjointed syntax, the apparent "madness" of the tumble of words—are laid against an equally firmly stressed sensuousness of subject and language. It is Williams's strategy for expressing the sensuousness of the local *and* the "local conditions" that have caused the neglect of the native landscape. Again it is Gris's demand for the "basic idea" directed by "an emotion" characteristic of "the aesthetic outlook of the period." Or as Williams wrote of Poe, "Heeding more the local necessities, the harder structural imperatives—by standing off to SEE instead of forcing [oneself] too close" (*IAG,* 228–29). The "cold" element, the "crudity," is essential for Williams. In Poe's tales he found the

> quality of skill in observation, their heat, local verity, being *overshadowed* only by the detached, the abstract, the cold philosophy of their joining together; a method springing so freshly from the local conditions which determine it, by their emphasis of firm crudity and lack of coordinated structure, as to be worthy of most painstaking study. (*IAG,* 231)

The difference between Williams and Rosenfeld in this regard marks one of the major differences between *Al Que Quiere*! and *Spring and All.* In poem XI of *Spring and All,* the poet's aloofness from the world around him allows him to bring the "structural imperatives" of a local scene together.

> In passing with my mind
> on nothing in the world
>
> but the right of way
> I enjoy on the road by
>
> virtue of the law--
> I saw
>
> an elderly man who
> smiled and looked away
>
> to the north past a house—
> a woman in blue
>
> who was laughing and
> leaning forward to look up
>
> into the man's half
> averted face
>
> and a boy of eight who was
> looking at the middle of
>
> the man's belly
> at a watchchain—

The nature of the relationships between the particulars is complex, although they all radiate from the "I saw" that initiates the pattern. Are man, woman, and boy momentarily joined in response to some event external to all three? Or are the man and woman so responding, while the boy responds to the man? Or is the man responding to the boy, and the woman to the man? There are other possibilities, but the point is that *all* these possibilities coexist at once. The signs that would normally give us clues to the relationships—of the individuals to each other, and of the cause and effect of responses—do not follow the conventional shorthand of visual delineation. What is the man smiling at? Why is he looking away? Why does the woman laugh? Why does she look at his face? Is the boy looking at the man's belly or his watchchain, and why? Is the woman "leaning forward to look up" only at the man, or at the man and the boy? What is significant here, and what is chance? The relationships overlap, expressing the unifying possibilities perceived by the artist, and translated into a composition that leaves this potential unconstrained. The aloofness allows the poet to leave his scene a "nameless spectacle," —"untamed" (Poem XIII) by names. Perception and poem both contain multiple possibilities of relationship, as fecund with potential as the encounter that concludes the lines.

> The supreme importance
> of this nameless spectacle
>
> sped me by them
> without a word—
>
> Why bother where I went?
> for I went spinning on the
>
> four wheels of my car
> along the wet road until
>
> I saw a girl with one leg
> over the rail of a balcony
>   (*Imag*, 119–20)

In "American Painting," Rosenfeld offers John Marin's "complete harmonious release" in contrast to what he sees as the trepidation of painters such as Hartley.[33] But for Williams, Marin's effusions are the "skyscraper soup" of Poem IX. And as noted earlier, when interviewed by Emily Farnham he compared Marin's formlessness unfavorably with Demuth's sense of structure. Hartley complained similarly in his *Adventures in the Arts* that Marin's work did not take into account the "important essentials" of "spatial existence and spatial relationships" that characterize modern art. Like Williams, he thought Marin's work undisciplined. As Kandinsky always insisted, spontaneity is no justification for formlessness.

In a mellow "Appreciation" of Marin written in 1955 after the painter's death Williams noted that the two were never close, although they "met and understood each other completely" (*ARI*, 229). It is possible to date Williams's probable first meeting with the painter through a letter from Marin amongst the poet's papers at Buffalo.

> My dear Doctor Williams
>   I have received your letter and am sure it too would give me pleasure to have you come up and see me. Tomorrow I go for an operation of the tonsils, later I'll call you up or drop you a line when we can meet.
>   Most sincerely
>   John Marin[34]

The background to this 1922 letter is an "Autobiographical Note" by Marin in *Manuscripts*, in which he mentions being born in Rutherford.[35] (The coincidence was one Williams always mentioned when writing of the painter.)

However Williams and Rosenfeld differed over the merits of individual painters, or the kind of art necessary to give full expression to local conditions, they saw themselves allied in the common cause of furthering native American expression. Through Rosenfeld, Williams contributed to the *American Caravan* anthologies in the late twenties and early thirties, and also to the *America and Alfred Stieglitz* volume. Rosenfeld included an essay on Williams in his *Port of New York,* praising the poet's use of local material. (In Rosenfeld's essay almost all the citations are from *Al Que Queire!* and there are none from *Spring and All.*) Williams in turn wrote an essay in tribute after the critic's death, commending his fidelity to the cause of the arts. In private, their attitudes towards each other were affectionately patronizing, Rosenfeld writing to Kreymborg of meeting "the mad hatter from Rutherford," and Williams telling McAlmon "I liked Paul, an old bumbling ass of a guy but nobody's dupe."[36]

In "American Painting" Rosenfeld had classed Demuth as "an exquisite and . . . limited talent" and merely listed Sheeler without discussing his paintings, but Sheeler and Demuth were the two American painters who most interested Williams through the 1920s.[37] In the work of these two painters Williams found what he admired in Gris, a detached treatment of the object that, while retaining the object's recognizability, translated its structural integrity into the compositional patterns of art. Writing of Sheeler, Williams termed this quality "The abstract . . . left by the artist integral with its native detail" (*ARI,* 143)

Demuth and Sheeler, responding to the innovations of the Dadaists, in particular the work of Duchamp and Picabia, and also to the articles of *L'Espirit Nouveau,* developed a strategy to incorporate the structure of mechanical and industrial objects into their compositions. The sharp linear patterns of these canvases contrast with the mass of the structures being diagrammed, a painterly equivalent to the contrast in Williams's poems between the "edge" of detail and syntax, and the sensuousness of subject.

Sheeler was closely associated with the Arensburg group, but Williams did not meet him until 1923, through the introduction of their mutual friend Maxwell Josephson. Sheeler's clear, dry, geometrically simplified paintings of factories, mills, and barns are more severe than Demuth's. Williams's account of Marianne Moore's use of words could be translated into an account of Sheeler's use of line.

With Miss Moore a word is a word most when it is separated out by science, treated with acid to remove the smudges, washed, dried and placed right side up on a clean surface. Now one may say that this is a word. Now it may be used, and how?

> It may be used not to smear it again with thinking (the attachments of thought) but in such a way that it will remain scrupulously itself, clean perfect, unnicked beside other words in parade. There must be edges. This casts some light I think on the simplicity of design in much of Miss Moore's work. (*Imag*, 318)

The word must be divorced from "the attachment of thought," and painterly composition from the conventions associated with "realistic" reproduction. To achieve this, for Williams, is to enter the realm of imagination, Gris's "detached" world, the world without "attachments" of a Moore poem, that "world" that Sheeler's "best pictures take us most wholly into" (*ARI*, 145), and the "WORLD" that "IS NEW" of *Spring and All* (*Imag*, 95). Williams's discussions of the move into this realm all emphasize the creative risk inherent in the necessary discarding of the safety net of conventional pattern. In the essay on Moore he writes of this move as "the unbridled leap" (*Imag*, 320). In *Spring and All*, the strategy behind *Kora in Hell* is described as "letting life go completely" (*Imag*, 116). There is always this risk in confronting the world of imagination; in *Spring and All*, "A terrific confusion has taken place. No man knows whither to turn" (*Imag*, 96). And the concept is distilled into a central motif in *Paterson*, "the unbridled leap" into the Passaic exercising a haunting fascination on generation upon generation of inhabitants of the city.

Within the "NEW" world of imagination objects are familiar, yet also transformed. The importance of this quality to Williams's thinking is revealed again and again in his admiration for Sheeler, Gris and Moore. Sheeler "sees the universal in our midst, with his eyes, and makes it up for us in detail from those things we know" (*ARI*, 142). Marianne Moore's difficult work has "recognizable edges" (*Imag*, 318), while a "fault" of Williams's improvisations "is their dislocation of sense, often complete" (*Imag*, 117). Williams praises Gris for using "forms common to experience" (*Imag*, 107).

In Williams's poetry, this demand for the "recognizable" dictates his choice of vocabulary, subject, and allusion, but the apparent recognizability is always accompanied by complicating factors that emphasize the translation of the familiar into the realm of art. The poems of *Spring and All* are often difficult, their levels of meaning complex, but they are almost all concerned with "recognizable" subjects. The first poem describes the poet's route to work, for example. The second a native flower. And so it continues, the succeeding poems taking their detail from the local landscape, local people, familiar objects and flowers. But this familiarity is set against the unfamiliarity of their context in the word-construction of a poem.

Similarly the chapters of *In the American Grain* are concerned with the figures of school-room history, but here the new context is the directness with which the lives and concerns of these figures are faced. The comfortable distancing of historical narrative is removed. The patterns of syntax are shaped by the "imperatives" of the subject, released from those "attachments of thought," locked-in patterns, that cloud the real significance of the historical moment. Sometimes this patterning is visual. Williams told Edith Heal: "The Tenochtitlan chapter was written in big square paragraphs like Inca masonry. I admired the massive walls of fitted masonry—no plaster—just fitted boulders" (*IWWP,* 42). In other chapters Williams reprints the "familiar" figures' own word patterns, and in others addresses the reader in a pastiche of their style. The format constantly changes; the "recognizable" always appears in an innovative context.

There is a similar effect in the "recognizable" vocabulary of the poems in *Spring and All*. The vocabulary and syntax are pared down as drastically as Gris's and Sheeler's designs, but the familiar is presented within the unfamiliar context of compositional pattern. This effect can occur within a single line:

> Drunk with goats or pavements
> (Poem V, *Imag,* 102)

or within a stanza:

> Waves of steel
> from
> swarming backstreets
> shell
> of coral
> inventing
> electricity—
> (Poem XIII, *Imag,* 125)

> cutting my
> life with
> sleep to trim
> my hair—
> (Poem XIV, *Imag,* 126)

or through the juxtaposition of apparently disparate images over a number of stanzas:

> What is the end
> to insects
> that suck gummed
> labels?

          for this is eternity
          through its
          dial we discover
          transparent tissue
          on a spool

          But the stars
          are round
          cardboard
          with a tin edge

          and a ring
          to fasten them
          to a trunk
          for the vacation—
                    (Poem XII, *Imag,* 124)

The "descent" structure so central to much of Williams's work is also "recognizable" in that he insisted it was one of the universal myths "far back in the psychic history of all races" containing "basic elements that can be comprehended and used with new force."[38] It is also familiar in being a constant pattern in nature, art, and history. Plants thrust down roots in order to blossom. The artist discovers the power of imagination in the "hell" of his despair (as in *Kora in Hell, Sour Grapes, Spring and All, Paterson* and numerous individual poems). Williams discovers the pattern in his history of the "Others" group, and in *In the American Grain* (*SL,* 33; *IAG,* 212–25).[39]

Many of the allusions in *Spring and All* are familiar. There are no footnotes, as in Eliot's *The Waste Land,* no esoteric classical references, but the familiar here, as with the other "recognizable" levels of *Spring and All,* is always complicated by the new context.[40]

Spring and All is dedicated to Charles Demuth. With Hartley having joined the exodus to Europe, Demuth was Williams's one painterly intimate remaining in the United States. Their correspondence in the early twenties testifies to their closeness. In 1921 Demuth sent Williams a book on Matisse, and the following year apparently introduced him to the poems of Emily Dickinson. Through his friend, Williams was permitted to view Dr. Albert Barnes's extensive private collection of modern paintings at Merion.[41]

However, Demuth's feelings about being out of the Parisian melee could be as ambivalent as Williams's own. A letter he wrote to Stieglitz two days after returning to Lancaster from Europe breathes the kind of grim determination to turn circumstances to advantage that marks Williams's letters to Pound at this time. The European trip "was all very wonderful, but I must work, here. Had I stayed in France when I went to it for the first time, by now I would be into it. . . . New York is something which Europe is not—and I feel of that something, awful as most of it is."[42]

Williams responded to the precisionist elements in Demuth's art that he also admired in Sheeler's. In 1920 he purchased Demuth's *End of the Parade—Coatesville, Pa.* (1920) from the Daniel Gallery and one of Demuth's flower studies, *Tuberoses,* in 1922. The connection between *Tuberoses* and Poem II of *Spring and All* has often been noticed. Demuth's watercolor sets the sharply-edged contours of the petals and flowers against the solid mass of leaves, earth, and flower-pots. The flowers' connection with the earth is strongly emphasized—there are three overlapping pots in the painting—and their mass frames the flowers, providing context, contrast, and the demarcation of compositional space. This is Williams's poem:

> Pink confused with white
> flowers and flowers reversed
> take and spill the shaded flame
> darting it back
> into the lamp's horn
>
> petals aslant darkened with mauve
>
> red where in whorls
> petal lays its glow upon petal
> round flamegreen throats
>
> petals radiant with transpiercing light
> contending
>   above
> the leaves
> reaching up their modest green
> from the pot's rim
>
> and there, wholly dark, the pot
> gay with rough moss
>
>   (*Imag,* 96)

Williams published his poem under a number of different titles. As well as its numerical designation in *Spring and All,* it was variously called "The Hothouse Plant," "The Pot of Primroses," and finally "The Pot of Flowers." As in Demuth's watercolor, the "petals radiant with transpiercing light" are set in opposition to the solidity of the leaves and earth. The lines:

> contending
>   above

are both a visual and a semantic pivot to the poem, Williams's patterning emphasizing the poem's status as an arrangement of words.

Demuth shared with Williams and Hartley, and many of the modernist painters in New York and Paris, an interest in vaudeville. At this period both cities saw a number of collaborations by painters, poets, producers, designers and musicians on music hall, cabaret, opera and ballet productions. The New York avant-garde viewed vaudeville as iconoclastic and uniquely American. *The Dial* regularly carried vaudeville reviews, Hartley devoted a number of essays to the subject, and it provided the theme for a number of Demuth's paintings. Apart from disregarding moral and theatrical conventions, vaudeville, like dance, offered a parallel to the modern artists' strategy: the resolution of contending forces into a balanced expressiveness of line.

Hartley's essay "A Charming Equestrienne" praises the variety performer May Wirth. "She is mistress of a very difficult art" yet "like all fine artists, she has brushed away from sight all aspects of labour, and presents you, with astounding ease, the apparent easiness of the thing."[43] In Poem V of *Spring and All* Williams alludes to Hartley's essay, contrasting the emotional overlay of the pathetic fallacy with performances that allow emotion and personality to be expressed through compositional pattern.

> That is why boxing matches and
> Chinese poems are the same—That is why
> Hartley praises Miss Wirt [*sic*]
>
> There is nothing in the twist
> of the wind but—dashes of cold rain
>   (*Imag,* 103)[44]

Williams's most ambitious poem on a vaudeville theme, "When Fresh, It Was Sweet" from *The Dial* of December 1922, is not directly concerned with American vaudeville. Apparently omitted from his *Collected Poems* in error, the poem records Williams's response to a performance of *Katinka* by Nakita Balieff's Chauve-Souris, or Bat, Company. The Moscow troupe appeared in New York through much of 1922. Contemporary critics noted the blend of the esoteric and the popular in their performances, the atmosphere being that of a club or cabaret, while the humor was broad and primitive. The reviewers found parallels with vaudeville and with the primitive movement in the fine arts.

In Williams's poem dance and vaudeville unite. The choreographer's success stems from a careful, passionate attention to particulars that are "translated" by him into the patterns of his art:

          the vision
predominates. Removed from the intimate
it is all intimate, closely observed
to be deftly translated to the stage—

The poem itself follows the strategy, the particulars of the performance translated into the rhythms of word pattern:

        Here life's exquisite diversity
its tenderness
ardour of spirits
find that in which they may move—

All enters—Katinka dances
The father blinks
The mother severely stares
—hey la!
we all laugh together—Life has us
by the arm.

Katinka dies by bending
her body down in a crouch about her knees
there she stays panting from
the exertion of dancing—

Through the patterns of the containing design,

The *ensemble* is felt
above the detail; the music goes
free of the fact   [Williams's emphasis][45]

These lines could also serve as a summary of Williams's intention in *Spring and All*—prose arguments interspersed with twenty-seven poems, but an overreaching design that "is felt / above the detail." Williams always regarded the prose text as an integral part of the book. In the first years of his association with James Laughlin, in the early 1930s, Williams twice asked for the "full text" of *Spring and All* to be printed.[46] Writing to Louis Untermeyer in 1924, he told him "Sour Grapes is not my latest book but the newer stuff is not suited for anthology purposes I am certain."[47] (Ironically, *Spring and All*'s "The Red Wheelbarrow" is by far Williams's most anthologized piece!)

In two reviews that Williams wrote around this time, of books by McAlmon and Marianne Moore, he had a good deal to say about structure. His discussions, and the painterly analogies he uses, cast a helpful light upon his own intentions in *Spring and All*. He describes McAlmon's technique in his collection of stories *A Hasty Bunch* as "to transcribe freely the immediate contact between his intelligence and the thing perceived."

> Every part of the picture is a direct observation presented as an integer; the consequent feeling being that of the building up of a definite material construction; a construction rising above the hackneyed quality of the fact itself. . . .
> Here is a cold, modern style, bred of an attack capable of absorbing, not from a window but from the round of a circle in the open, anything in modern life pressing upon it; it is a method that is broad enough, closely enough knit, and above everything else sufficiently aloof within itself to withstand, without a structural tremor, the modern impact as no flimsy extrinsic literary invention can ever do.[48]

The particulars of modern life are "absorbed"—"not from a window," the framed conventions of illusionist art now cast aside, but "from the round of a circle," absorbed into a structure whose self-referential patterns center upon compositional concerns. In the imaginative world of *Spring and All*, "Through the orderly sequences of unmentionable time EVOLUTION HAS REPEATED ITSELF FROM THE BEGINNING. . . . It is spring. That is to say, it is approaching THE BEGINNING" (*Imag*, 93, 94). The resulting self-referential form of in *Spring and All* is "broad enough" for some readers to see the arrangement of poems and prose as merely random, while also "closely enough knit" for relationships within the text to be diagrammed. For Williams, these relationships stem from the inner dynamics of the text, not from the imposition upon the material of some "flimsy, extrinsic literary invention." The pattern's self-referential status makes it "immovable in structure," able to "record finely" such eclectic detail as "wind, earthquakes / in Manchuria, a / partridge / from dry leaves," the spirit of a baseball crowd, or the exhortations of an IRT poster.

The mathematical term "integer" that Williams uses in discussing *A Hasty Bunch* is particularly appropriate with regard to *Spring and All*. The poems are numbered, not titled—each poem a "part of the picture," while retaining the integrity of a whole number. *Spring and All*, like *Kora in Hell*, contains twenty-seven sections, the number, as discussed in chapter 4, displaying mathematically the "broad" yet "closely enough knit" qualities that Williams demanded of the modern method. The self-referential nature of the system of mathematics suggests Williams's compositional concerns, a self-contained scheme demanding full recognition of the formal properties of its individual elements as the first step towards achieving patterns utilizing those properties.

In a 1925 review of Marianne Moore's *Observations*, Williams makes clear the place of mathematics within his concept of "imagination."

A course in mathematics would not be wasted on a poet, or a reader of poetry, if he remember no more from it than the geometric principle of the intersection of loci: from all angles lines converging and crossing establish points. He might carry it further and say in his imagination that apprehension perforates at places, through to understanding—as white is at the intersection of blue and green and yellow and red. (*Imag*, 311)

Both *Spring and All* and *In the American Grain* are replete with images of entry and penetration, as well as themes which "converging and crossing establish points." "Good modern work," Williams continues in the Moore review,

far from being the fragmentary, neurotic thing its disunderstanders think it, is nothing more than work compelled by these conditions. It is a multiplication of impulses that by their several flights, crossing at all eccentric angles, *might* enlighten. As a phase, in its slightest beginning, it is more a disc pierced here and there by light; it is really distressingly broken up. But so does any attack seem at the moment of engagement, multiple units crazy except when viewed as a whole. (*Imag*, 312)

Similarly the significance of the distortions in modern painting can be realized "when viewed as a whole." The context in which to view Gris's overlapping objects in *The Open Window* is their status as pattern within an imaginative artifact constructed of paint and canvas. Poe's "surface of bizarre designs" assumes its correct significance when seen in terms of his imaginative response to "local causes" (*IAG*, 219). The poems of *Spring and All* also have to be seen within the context of their place in the book's patterns. Seen in context, such art displays that "essential and continuous organization" that Williams assailed the Dadaists for failing to realize in their art, as well as the "infinity of / combinations," looked to in Poem VI (*Imag*, 104).

The themes of time and speed are also important elements in Williams's painterly parallels in the McAlmon and Moore reviews. The compositional patterns of a painting can be viewed through one continuous visual experience (another aspect of Williams's phrase "the round of a circle"). The spectator's grasp of the work's design is a simultaneous recognition of the composition's "particulars" and their place in the overall pattern. These are the terms in which Williams praised Moore's work. She manages "to separate the poetry from the subject entirely" through "rapidity of movement. A poem such as 'Marriage' is an anthology of transit. It is a pleasure that can be held firm only by moving rapidly from one thing to the next" (*Imag*, 313).

The poems of *Spring and All* are marked by rapid movement. Delays of punctuation are largely avoided; the most frequent mark used is the dash. The poems' line-breaks rarely coincide with the termination of a phrase or idea, so that the eye is hurriedly moved on to the next line. Detail is piled upon detail, and grammatical elements that would clarify the direction of the syntax are held back. The overall effect is to speed up reading, while at the same time emphasizing the equal status of every word and detail by demanding that careful attention be paid at every stage.

The book's interrupted prose sections and back-to-back grouping of poems also invite a hurried, breathless reading. Many of the paragraphs are a single sentence or a half-sentence, and sentences are begun and discarded. Some ideas are urgently repeated, while others are dropped before being completely expressed. Shakespeare becomes "S" or "W. S.," as if Williams did not have time to write the name out in full. The prose text is referred to at one point as "these few notes jotted down in the midst of the action, under distracting circumstances—to remind myself . . . of the truth" (*Imag,* 98).

Williams used the title *Go Go* for a selection of the *Spring and All* poems published in the United States in 1923, drawing attention to his demand for the instantaneous apprehension of design. Explaining the title to the publisher, Monroe Wheeler, Williams insisted, "It is 'go go' and keep right on going through the back cover and everything else. . . ."[49]

The design of *Spring and All* that Williams wanted recognized instantaneously is a complex one. On one level *Spring and All* may be read as proceeding straightforwardly. The poems are numbered consecutively from I to XXVII (although Poem VII is actually unnumbered). Poem I concerns the onset of spring, the first growth of new roots, and the concluding Poem XXVII describes a flower in full bloom. The prose can also be read as a straightforward manifesto. It begins by insisting that modern art exists on its own terms as a product of the modern imagination. It then discusses the dangers of stale symbolism, and the way such artists as Gris, Shakespeare, and Cézanne capture the essence of the particular by lifting it to the imagination. The argument then moves on to the difference between prose and the new free verse—with Marianne Moore's work as example—and concludes by emphasizing the need to liberate words from "specified meanings" through "transposition into another medium, the imagination" (*Imag,* 150).

But another aspect of the design comes into play when we consider the mathematical qualities of the number 27. Williams had already used these qualities in the improvisations, their "concealed construction" (Kandinsky's term) paralleling the pattern of threes that make up twenty-seven. The poems of *Spring and All* can be loosely grouped into nine sets of three in terms of their themes. Poems I–III announce spring, the rooting of flowers, and the farmer's anticipation of a future harvest. Poems

IV–VI concern infertility and various kinds of failure. Poems VII–IX have as a common theme the "obsolete"—the sentimental associations of the rose, J. P. Morgan's attitude to art, and the remembered passion of a long-dead affair. By contrast, Poems X–XII present particular objects freshly encountered—litter on a garbage heap, a group of people, and a "red paper box." XIII to XV are the poems displaying the most extreme dislocation of syntax. Their common theme is the compositional pattern that "knits peace" out of their contending particulars. Poems XVI–XVIII are all concerned with "the pure products of America," its people. "Primitive" motifs unite Poems XIX–XXI—the satyrs of XIX, the sea-gods of XX, and the gypsy of XXI. With XXII–XXIV we are in a pastoral setting, while the final group, XXV–XXVII, concentrates on particulars of modern American life traditionally considered outside the realm of art: advertising, baseball, and the common weed, the black-eyed susan.

This is one way to diagram the design of *Spring and All*. Another is to consider each poem as an outgrowth of its immediately surrounding prose discussion. As Williams puts it at one point: "Prose has to do with the fact of an emotion; poetry has to do with the dynamization of emotion into a separate form. This is the force of imagination" (*Imag*, 133). The poems can thus be read as a "dynamization . . . into a separate form" of the 'facts' discussed in the prose. The first prose pages present a new world, of America and of the imagination. Poem I describes the potential available upon entrance to that world, and Poem II part of the new landscape (the plant native to Mexico, Demuth's composition *Tuberoses* native to the imagination). The prose acknowledges that holding to the truth "that design is a function of the imagination . . . is a hard battle" (*Imag*, 98). In Poem III the farmer, a "composing / antagonist," designs the coming harvest in his imagination. Poem IV treats of a spurious design— possibly a store window display—that rests upon prior association for its meaning, while Poems V and VI acknowledge the difficulty of creating a design that has reference only to its own internally generated patterns and associations. The prose around Poems VII, VIII, and IX continues with the insistence upon the need for work that achieves an autonomous existence, that does not rely for meaning upon relationships habitually perceived in nature or in the past. Gris's work is held up as an example, and Poem VII celebrates his rejuvenation of the rose. Poem VIII deplores J. P. Morgan's association of "art" only with old masters, and also his assumption that artistic value is synonymous with market value. Poem IX treats of some false romantic associations of the poet's own. Poems X and XI mirror the prose discussion of that "condition of imaginative suspense" (*Imag*, 120) which allows the artist to discard conventional ways of thinking and seeing, and to realize the compositional potential of particulars in newly realized patterns. The prose moves on to discuss the way Shakespeare used characters and the "objects of his world . . . with understanding to make his inventions" (*Imag,* 122). Poems XII–XVIII show Williams similarly using *his* world of objects, landscape, and people. The primitive "force" behind "all human activity" (*Imag,* 135) is delineated in the satyric teenagers of Poem XIX, the sacrificial lovemaking of Poem XX, the primeval gypsy of Poem XXI, and the gardener of Poem XXII. The free-ranging patterning of particulars in Poems XXIII and XXIV demonstrate that "crystallization of the imagination" (*Imag,* 140) which distinguishes poetry from the clarity of prose. The prose discussion of Marianne Moore's control of the direction of words in her work is matched by two poems on the theme of direction: the IRT train's charge to Long Island, and "the crowd at the ball game / . . . moved uniformally." Finally, the summation of the prose themes is followed by a poem that draws on some of the key motifs of the earlier verse: flowers, crowds, and farmers, for its summation.

Spring and All can also be diagrammed in terms of key metaphors that appear and reappear in the verse. Important among these are the metaphor of light and dark contending (in 10 of the poems), the "primitive" theme (in 11 poems), the flower and leaves imagery (10 poems), and the sensual imagery (10 poems). We can also trace such patterns as "the lamp's horn" of Poem II, the "cornucopia / of glass" of Poem IV, and the "horned lilac blossoms" of Poem XIX.

The 27 poems are also patterned according to Williams's "descent" myth. The descent, as always in Williams's work, results in the rescue of the female principle of the imagination, Kora, from her subterranean imprisonment. For Williams, this is to tap the center, the core, of that imaginative power that gives shape and substance to the artist's composition.

The descent pattern of *Spring and All* can be outlined this way. Poem I describes an entrance to a new landscape, and Poem II a "particular" of that landscape (the new world of America and "the imagination"). In Poem III the "artist figure of the farmer" takes up the challenge to produce a harvest from the potential of this spring. Poems IV, V, and VI demonstrate the difficulty of this challenge. IV describes a false composition, V a battle to dismiss the associations of the pathetic fallacy, and VI marks the intent to write without the constraints of convention and association that would deny the poem the right to determine its own patterns. Poem VII begins the task, rehabilitating the hackneyed rose, while Poem VIII asserts the suitability of all material of the moment as potential subject matter for the modern poem, not, Poem IX asserts, sentimental associations rooted in the past, but the immediately observed particulars of X–XIII.

This is success, but also the beginning of the descent. Poem XIV introduces the theme of death, and Poem XV of night and decay. However, this descent is also creative, for

> destruction and creation
> are simultaneous . . .
>
> woe is translatable
> to joy if light becomes
> darkness and darkness
> light, as it will
> > *(Imag, 127)*

Poem XVI dramatizes a fear of dying, "Elysian slobber"—the mark of the lower world—upon the dying old woman. The music that will rescue Kora and "soothe / the savage beast" is the Negro jazz of Poem XVII. Here America's primitives realize native expression, but there is a sharp contrast in Poems XVII and XVIII that points out the potential and the tragedy of America's "hell." As in Poe's work, creativity is not far from madness.

> Man
> gimme the key
>
> and lemme loose—
> I make 'em crazy
>
> with my harmonies—
> > (Poem XVII, *Imag,* 130)
>
> The pure products of America
> go crazy—
> > (Poem XVIII, *Imag,* 131)

Poem XIX continues the theme of America's potential energies. Poem XX takes us to the sea, the playing of the gods in the depths of water. The poem fuses death and life, male and female, actual and mythological. The sea is a place of death and rebirth, of romantic clichés and the beginning of a language washed clean and made new. The depths, "where the night is deep" are attractive, but

> Underneath the sea where it is dark
> there is no edge

The "edge" is where shore meets sea.

> Deeply the wooing that penetrated
> to the edge of the sea
> returns in the plash of the waves—
> *(Imag,* 137)

"It is imperative that we *sink,*" Williams argues in *In the American Grain.* However, this return to origins is always in order to see the American particular anew, it is not an end in itself. With a glance at Eliot and Pound, he continues, "But from a low position it is impossible to answer those who know all the Latin and some of the Sanskrit names, much French and perhaps one or two other literatures." The poet must "come up from under" *(IAG,* 214–15). Similarly the concluding pages of *Paterson* IV insist:

> The sea is not our home—
>   — not our home! It is NOT
> our home.
> *(Pat,* 201–2)

And so in *Spring and All,* after Poem XX the poet returns to shore, to the new Eden landscape where

> one day in Paradise
> a Gypsy
>
> smiled
> to see the blandness
>
> of the leaves—
> so many
>
> so lascivious
> and still
> (Poem XXI, *Imag,* 137–38)

The similarity between this poem and the final page of the Columbus chapter in *In the American Grain* is striking. Columbus has also come from the sea, taking the risk of leaving the old behind.

> Bright green trees, the whole land so green that it is a pleasure to look on it. Gardens of the most beautiful trees I ever saw. . . .
>   During that time I walked among the trees which was the most beautiful thing which I had ever seen. . . . *(IAG,* 26)

Poem XXII stays with gardens, emphasizing the primitive necessities required for cultivation of the harvest that will fulfill spring's potential.

The poem also emphasizes the new world of patterns and relationships within the world of the imagination. These objects are not, however, those particulars of modern life that the poem sequence must absorb. We are still in the realm of those "basic elements that can be comprehended and used with new force [that are] far back in the psychic history of all races."[50]

Poems XXIII and XXIV are still set within the darkness of hell, but

>   now at last
>   the truth's aglow
>
>   with devilish peace
>   (Poem XXIII, *Imag,* 142)

Poem XXIV confirms that the condition postulated earlier in Poem VI is now realized: "everything / and nothing / are synonymous," language and self renewed in a world of imaginative potential that disregards the authority of any previous patterns.

>   The leaves embrace
>   in the trees
>
>   it is a wordless
>   world
>
>   without personality
>   I do not
>
>   seek a path

The renewal out of the depths acknowledges the multidirectional possibilities contained in the poems, and in the overall design of the book.

>   I ascend
>
>   through
>   a canopy of leaves
>
>   and at the same time
>   I descend
>   (*Imag,* 143)

Poem XXV is the ascent, in the full roar of a subway charging into the open. It is also a visual ascent, from south to north on the subway map. And this transition from darkness to light absorbs the particulars of modern life—speed and the city—within it. Poem XXVI also utilizes material from modern American life—a baseball game. But this modern composite of particulars, the "detail" that "is moved uniformally," also contains all crowds, the universal in the local. Crowd and poem are identified.

> it smiles grimly
> its words cut—
>
> *(Imag,* 148)

for the poem is also a collection of particulars, words, given direction by the poet. Both poem and crowd contain all history; both are "permanent," and both are "without" the overlay of "thought."

In Poem XXVII the black-eyed susan—"rich orange / round the purple core"—is in full bloom, the full expression of the rescued Kora/"core." Suitably the flower is a weed. In *In the American Grain* Williams warns "those who come up from under will have a mark on them that invites scorn" *(IAG,* 215).

> Black eyed susan
> rich orange
> round the purple core
>
> the white daisy
> is not
> enough
>
> Crowds are white
> as farmers
> who live poorly
>
> But you
> are rich
> in savagery—
>
> Arab
> Indian
> dark woman

The poem unites light (the first three stanzas) with dark (the final two). It insists that the flowering of the poem and the book is dependent upon being rooted in the descent that the whole sequence has enacted. The poem is also a paean to Kora herself, the dark woman whose fertility has given birth to the poem and to the book that the poem completes.

All of these patterns within *Spring and All* come together in the "moment" of apprehension that marks the realization of its multiple directions. But there is one other important pattern within the book, the pattern that marks *Spring and All* as the personal expression of its creator. The "design . . . of the IMAGINATION" *(Imag,* 98) that *Spring and All* records incorporates its author's response to being an embattled modernist writer forced to remain in an America that has driven so many of its finest artists to flee to Europe. The "contending forces" that Williams recognized within his own "design in life" become part of the contending forces that make up the design of *Spring and All*. In the first sentence of the book he despairs of finding a reader. The "Descent" chapter of *In the American Grain* acknowledges that "those who come up from under . . . will be recognized only from *abroad* (Williams's emphasis) (*IAG*, 215). *Spring and All* was printed in France, and such close friends as Pound and Kenneth Burke did not see it. McAlmon, Hartley and Pound were all in Europe, and Williams often yearned to join them. Robert McAlmon's 1923 short-story "What is Left Undone" provides an insight to Williams's grim determination. In the story, Dr. Jim, a family doctor, is a thinly disguised Williams. At the end of a typically harassed day Dr. Jim sits down at his office desk, "wondering what he could do to express a wildness of revolt within him, a wildness of revolt against bodily weariness and emotional apathy towards all things occurring about him." He sits down to write a letter, "scribbling hastily," concluding with, "What is America? What are we for? Should we give up everything, and follow—but what, what? My head's spinning. . . ." But the doctor's final realization is that the "contending forces" of his daily life give shape to that life, to his art, and to his America. "Undressing tiredly," he tells his wife, "Being a doctor teaches one, all right, and it keeps the time occupied; and even in the so-called filth and chaos of it sometimes I begin to recognize a design in life. That finally is all there is, a pattern."[51]

Afterword

Williams continued to look to the visual arts as a source and parallel for his work for the rest of his life. Essays such as "An Afternoon with Tchelitchew" (1937, *ARI*, 119–23), "Walker Evans: American Photographs" (1938, *ARI*, 136–39), "E. E. Cummings's Paintings and Poems" (1954, *ARI*, 233–37), and "Brancusi" (1955, *ARI*, 246–54) document this continuing interest. It is found throughout the novels and poetry, from "Dev" Evans of *A Voyage to Pagany* (1928) exploring his responses to the achievements of France and Italy, to the late poem "Tribute to the Painters" which celebrates

> the knowledge of
> the tyranny of the image
> and how
>   men
> in their designs
>   have learned
>   to shatter it
>   (*PB*, 135–37)

and to the "Pictures from Breughel" sequence.

The direction of Williams's later work is towards a reconciliation with art of the past that allows this art to speak through the poet far more on its own terms than his earlier poetry would allow. The pressures of the past in the earlier work are shaped to a design that stresses the exigencies of the present, the urgent need for contemporary expression. In the later work, the past comes more to achieve an equal status with the present in the shaping of the poem, a resolution often marked by a return of that reflective quality that Williams had excised from *Kora in Hell* and *Spring and All*. Fine as much of this later verse is, it often lacks the dynamics of the conflicting, overlapping, internally generated patterns that charge *Spring and All* and give shape to its self-made, self-referential history. Nevertheless, the relationship of Williams's visual arts interests to this later work is an important subject in itself, and has been the focus of two recent discussions, Henry M. Sayre's, *The Visual Text of William Carlos Williams* (Champaign: Univ. of Illinois Press, 1983) and Dickran Tashjian's, *William Carlos Williams and the American Scene, 1920–1940* (Berkeley and New York: Univ. of Calif. Press and Whitney Museum of American Art, 1978). The reader interested in pursuing the story of the fertile collaboration outlined in this study is referred to these texts.

Notes

Preface

1. Ezra Pound, *The Letters of Ezra Pound, 1907–1941,* ed. D. D. Paige (New York: Harcourt, Brace, 1950), 4.

2. T. E. Hulme, "A Lecture on Modern Poetry," *Further Speculations,* ed. Sam Hynes (Minneapolis: Univ. of Minnesota Press, 1955), 73, 72.

Chapter 1

1. Emily Farnham, *Charles Demuth: Behind a Laughing Mask* (Norman: Univ. of Oklahoma Press, 1971), 48.

2. Emily Farnham, "Charles Demuth, His Life, Psychology, and Works," Diss. Ohio State 1959, 989.

3. Farnham, Diss., 444.

4. Farnham, *Behind a Laughing Mask,* 112.

5. Kandinsky's impact upon the American modernists has only recent ly been recognized. *See*: Sandra Gail Levin, "Wassily Kandinsky and the American Avant-Garde, 1912–1950," Diss. Rutgers 1976.

6. Farnham, Diss., 956–57.

7. Ezra Pound, "Edward Wadsworth, Vorticist," *The Egoist,* 1 (1914):306.

8. Williams, unpublished letter to Mrs. W. G. Williams, 18 April 1904, Williams Collection Za 221, Beinecke Rare Book and Manuscript Library, Yale.

9. Williams, unpublished letter to Norman Holmes Pearson, 20 Sept. 1957, Yale Za 221.

10. Williams, unpublished letters to Edgar Williams, 13 Oct. 1904, 21 Oct. 1908, Yale Za 221.

11. William Eric Williams, "The House," *WCWN* 5, No. 1 (Spring 1979):3.

12. Williams, unpublished letter to Edgar Williams, 21 Aug 1908, Yale Za 221. It would be five years before the museum purchased its first Cézanne, from the Armory Show.

13. Williams, unpublished letter to Edgar Williams, 6 April 1909, Yale Za 221.

14. Geoffrey H. Movius notes with reference to this description: "Williams had probably seen Turner's 'The Whale Ship' at the Metropolitan Museum in New York many times;

and it is likely that he also knew 'The Slave Ship,' purchased by the Boston Museum of Fine Arts in 1899." "Caviar and Bread: Ezra Pound and William Carlos Williams, 1902–1914," *JML,* 5 (1976):392.

15. Pound, "Fragment to W.C.W.'s Romance," *Collected Early Poems of Ezra Pound,* ed. Michael John King (New York: New Directions, 1976), 247.

16. Pound, *Letters,* 6.

17. Ezra Pound, unpublished letter to Isabel Pound, 12 Mar. 1910, Paige Carbons, Beinecke Rare Book and Manuscript Library, Yale.

18. *MR,* 3 (1962):324.

19. Letter to Isabel Pound, 7 Jan. 1909, rpt. in *Ezra Pound and the Visual Arts,* ed. Harriet Zinnes (New York: New Directions, 1980), 287.

20. This is the *Poetry Review* version; *CEP* has some changes in punctuation, *The Poetry Review* 1 (1912):482.

21. Pound, *Collected Early Poems,* 197, 71.

22. *The Poetry Review,* 1 (1912):483.

23. For idealized ladies in Pound see his " 'Portrait" and " 'Fair Helena' by Rackham," *Collected Early Poems,* 115–16.

24. *The Poetry Review,* 1 (1912):483–84.

25. *Imag,* 137; *Pat,* 203, *IAG,* 26.

26. H. D., *End to Torment* (New York: New Directions, 1979), 23.

27. Pound, *Letters,* 4.

28. Ezra Pound, *The Spirit of Romance* (1910; rpt. New York: New Directions, 1952), 154.

29. T. E. Hulme, "A Lecture on Modern Poetry," 72–73.

30. Pound, *Letters,* 10. The Tate Gallery, London, held a Whistler Exhibition from July to October 1912.

31. Ezra Pound, "A Selection from *The Tempers,*" *Poetry Review,* 1 (1912):481.

32. "Patria Mia," *New Age,* 24 Oct 1912, 612; reprinted in *Selected Prose 1909–1965* (New York: New Directions, 1973), 117.

33. Quoted in Denys Sutton, *Nocturne: The Art of James McNeill Whistler* (London: Country Life, 1963), 49.

34. Vance and Whiteside appear in Pound's "Redondillas, or Something of That Sort" (1911).

> I praise God for a few royal fellows
> like Plarr and Fred Vance and Whiteside

Pound, *Collected Early Poems,* 216. Vance also appears in the first version of Canto II, *Poetry,* 10 (1917):187–88.

35. Ezra Pound, "Teacher's Mission," *English Journal (College Edition),* 23 (1934), 630; Pound, *Letters,* 51.

36. Ezra Pound, unpublished letter to Isabel Pound, 1911, Paige Carbons, Yale.

37. Marius De Zayas, "The New Art in Paris," *The Forum,* 45 (Feb. 1911): 181–85.

38. Ezra Pound, unpublished letters to Isabel Pound, 26 March 1911; 16 May 1911; to Homer Pound, May 1911, Paige Carbons, Yale.

39. Ezra Pound, "I Gather the Limbs of Osiris," *The New Age,* 22 Feb. 1912, 393; *Selected Prose,* 42.

40. Wyndham Lewis, "Editorial," *Blast,* No. 2 (July 1915):5.

Chapter 2

1. Ezra Pound, "A Few Don'ts by an Imagiste," *Poetry,* 1 (1913):200; *Literary Essays of Ezra Pound,* ed. T. S. Eliot (London: Faber, 1954), 4.

2. "A Few Don'ts," 199; *Literary Essays,* 3.

3. Ezra Pound, "Art Notes," *The New Age,* 21 Nov. 1918, 44; Zinnes, 86.

4. Yeats's verse reflects a similar shift with his 1914 volume *Responsibilities.* In "A Coat" he declares, "there's more enterprise / In walking naked."

5. Ezra Pound, "The Tempers," *The New Freewoman,* 1 (1913):227.

6. Ezra Pound, "How I Began," *T. P.'s Weekly,* 6 June 1913, 143.

7. Ezra Pound, "Vorticism," *Fortnightly Review,* 1 Sept. 1914, 461–71; reprinted in *Gaudier-Brzeska* (1916; New York: New Directions, 1970), 81–94.

8. Wassily Kandinsky, "Inner Necessity," trans. Edward Wadsworth, *Blast,* No. 1 (June 1914):119–25. Except where noted, all quotations from Kandinsky in this chapter are from this translation.

9. Ezra Pound, "The Renaissance," *Poetry,* 5 (1915):227; *Literary Essays,* 214.

10. Ezra Pound, "Arnold Dolmetsch," *The Egoist,* 4 (1917):104.

11. H. Gaudier-Brzeska, "Allied Artist's Association Ltd.," *The Egoist,* 1 (1914):231; *Gaudier-Brzeska,* 33.

12. Wyndham Lewis, "A Review of Contemporary Art," *Blast,* No. 2 (July 1915):40.

13. Ezra Pound, "Affirmations . . . II Vorticism," *The New Age,* 14 Jan. 1915, 278; Zinnes, 9.

14. "Wyndham Lewis, "Editorial," *Blast,* No. 2 (July 1915):5.

15. See Peter Selz, *German Expressionist Painting* (Berkeley: Univ. of Calif. Press, 1957), 9.

16. Ezra Pound, unpublished letter to Isabel Pound, 20 Jan 1914, Paige Carbons, Yale.

17. T. E. Hulme, "Modern Art and Its Philosophy," *Speculations,* ed. Herbert Read (New York: Harcourt, Brace, 1924), 82. In his *A Concise History of Modern Painting* (New York: Praeger, 1959), Read suggests some "parallels in literature" for "Worringer's

argument," singling out Joyce, Brecht, and "the verse forms of Ezra Pound, William Carlos Williams, and Boris Pasternack," 220.

18. *Speculations,* 84–86, 104, 103.

19. Ezra Pound, "The New Sculpture," *The Egoist,* 1 (1914):67–68; Zinnes, 179–82.

20. Ezra Pound, "The Caressability of the Greeks," *The Egoist,* 1 (1914):117; Zinnes, 186.

21. Ezra Pound, "Edward Wadsworth: Vorticist," *The Egoist,* 1 (1914):306–7; Zinnes, 190–93.

22. Ezra Pound, "Vortex: Pound," *Blast,* No. 1 (June 1914):153–54; Zinnes, 152.

23. "Affirmations . . . II Vorticism," 278; Zinnes, p. 9.

24. H. Gaudier-Brzeska, "Gaudier-Brzeska Vortex," *Blast,* No. 1 (June 1914):155–6; *Gaudier-Brzeska,* 20–24.

25. Ezra Pound, "The Later Yeats," *Poetry,* 4 (1914):68.

26. Ezra Pound, "Brancusi," *The Little Review,* 8, No. 1 (Autumn 1921):3; *Literary Essays,* 441.

27. "Affirmations . . . II Vorticism," 277; Zinnes, 6.

28. Ezra Pound, "Dubliners and Mr. James Joyce," *The Egoist,* 1 (1914):267; *Literary Essays,* 400.

29. In his painting Franz Marc investigated the way animals see the world in his attempts to move away from conventional pattern.

30. Ezra Pound, unpublished letter to William Carlos Williams, 26 Oct 1912, Poetry Collection of the Lockwood Memorial Library, SUNY Buffalo, F501; Pound, *Letters,* 27.

31. Williams, unpublished letters to Viola Jordan, 7 June 1914, 11 June 1914, Viola Baxter Jordan Papers, Beinecke Rare Book and Manuscript Library, Yale.

32. F. S. Flint, "The History of Imagism," *The Egoist,* 2 (1915):70.

33. *The New York Times,* 10 Feb. 1917, p. 10, col. 2.

34. Ezra Pound, unpublished letter to Homer Pound, Oct. 1915, Paige Carbons, Yale.

35. Ezra Pound, unpublished letter to Alfred Kreymborg, 1922, Kreymborg Papers, University of Virginia.

36. H. Gaudier-Brzeska, "Vortex Gaudier-Brzeska," *Blast,* No. 2 (July 1915):34; *Gaudier-Brzeska,* 27–28.

37. *The Egoist,* 1 (1914):308; *New Directions 16,* (New York: New Directions, 1957), 10–11.

38. *Others,* 2, No. 2 (Feb. 1916):139; *New Directions 16,* 10–11.

39. "The Great Sex Spiral, A Criticism of Miss Marsden's 'Lingual Psychology,' " *The Egoist,* 4 (1917):111.

40. As noted in Bram Dijkstra, *The Hieroglyphics of a New Speech: Cubism, Stieglitz, and the Early Poetry of William Carlos Williams* (Princeton: Princeton University Press, 1969), 60–63.

41. Ezra Pound, "Affirmations . . . III Jacob Epstein," *The New Age,* 21 Jan. 1915, 311.

42. "Gaudier-Brzeska Vortex," 155; *Gaudier-Brzeska*, 23.

43. Williams, "The Great Sex Spiral," III.

44. Fra Angelico's *Annunciation* is actually in San Marco, Florence; Dijkstra, *Hieroglyphics*, 60.

45. Just as "January Morning: Suite" recalls Whitman's "Crossing Brooklyn Ferry," this poem may recall his "To a Locomotive in Winter."

46. "Gaudier-Brzeska Vortex," 155; *Gaudier-Brzeska*, 23.

47. Wassily Kandinsky, *The Art of Spiritual Harmony*, trans. M. T. Sadler (London: Constable, 1914), 43.

Chapter 3

1. Alfred Stieglitz, unpublished letter to Ezra Pound, 3 Nov. 1915, Stieglitz Archive, Beinecke Rare Book and Manuscript Library, Yale.

2. Pound, *Letters*, 72.

3. Ezra Pound, unpublished letter to Alfred Stieglitz, 20 Dec. 1934, Stieglitz Archive, Yale.

4. Pound, *Letters*, 27; Alfred Kreymborg, *Troubadour* (New York: Boni and Liveright, 1925), 157.

5. Kreymborg, *Troubadour*, 112–15, 165–66, 203.

6. Paul Rosenfeld, unpublished letter to Alfred Kreymborg, 3 Dec. 1931, Kreymborg Papers, University of Virginia.

7. Alfred Kreymborg, "Stieglitz and '291'," *The Morning Telegraph* [New York], 14 June 1914, Sec. 2, p. 1.

8. Sherwood Anderson, "The New Note," *The Little Review*, 1, No. 1 (1914):23.

9. Ibn Gabirol, "My Friend, the Incurable," *The Little Review*, 1, No. 8 (1914):44.

10. Marsden Hartley, unpublished letter to Alfred Stieglitz, 1 Feb. 1917, Stieglitz Archive, Yale.

11. Willard Huntington Wright, "What is Modern Painting?" *The Forum Exhibition of Modern American Painters* (New York: Mitchell Kennerley, 1916), 13–16.

12. A. J. Eddy, *Cubists and Post-Impressionism* (Chicago: A. C. McClurg, 1914), 73.

13. Alfred Kreymborg, "The New Washington Square," *The Morning Telegraph*, 6 Dec. 1914, Sec. 2, p. 1.

14. *Others* 2, No. 2 (1916):155.

15. Wright, *Forum Exhibition*, 16–17.

16. *Rogue* 1, No. 6 (1915):18.

17. *The Blind Man*, No. 1 (April 1917):6.

18. "The Richard Mutt Case," *The Blind Man*, No. 2 (May 1917):5.

19. Williams, "America, Whitman, and the Art of Poetry," *The Poetry Review,* 8, No. 1 (1917):31.

20. Williams, "America, Whitman, and the Art of Poetry," 34, 33.

21. R. J. Coady, "The Indeps," *The Soil,* 1 (1917):202.

22. Williams, "America, Whitman, and the Art of Poetry," 35.

23. Ibid., 33.

24. Kreymborg, "Stieglitz and '291'," 1.

25. "Marsden Hartley," *Forum Exhibition,* no page.

26. *Camera Work,* No. 45 (1914):17.

27. Ibid., 23.

28. "Hartley Exhibition," *Camera Work,* No. 48 (1916):12.

29. Ibid., 59.

30. Charlotte Teller, "From Berlin," *The Little Review,* 3, No. 7 (1916):26. This article is not listed in the Hartley bibliography in Barbara Haskell, *Marsden Hartley* (New York: Whitney Museum of American Art/ New York Univ. Press, 1980), 194–208.

31. *The Egoist,* 1 (1914):307.

32. Williams, "The Great Sex Spiral, A Criticism of Miss Marsden's 'Lingual Psychology,' Chapter 1," *The Egoist,* 4 (1917):46.

33. Williams, "The Great Sex Spiral, A Criticism of Miss Marsden's 'Lingual Psychology'":III.

34. "Notes," *The Dial,* 2 Sept. 1915, 162.

35. *Twentieth Century Authors,* ed. J. Kunitz and Howard Haycroft (New York: H. W. Wilson, 1951), 42–43.

36. "The Author of Sanine," *The Dial,* 28 Oct. 1915, 365. Artsybashev's son, Boris, provided the illustrations for Kreymborg's 1927 *Funny-Bone Alley.*

37. *The Little Review,* 4, No. 1 (1917):70.

38. Ezra Pound, "Arnold Dolmetsch," 104.

39. *The Little Review,* 4, No. 8 (1917):45.

40. Williams, "America, Whitman, and the Art of Poetry," 36, 30.

Chapter 4

1. Williams, unpublished letter to Edmund Brown, 27 Jan. 1919, University of Virginia Collection.

2. Alanson Hartpence, unpublished letter to Williams, n.d., Buffalo, F214.

3. Quoted in John Lane, *Stuart Davis: Art and Art Theory* (Brooklyn, N.Y.: Brooklyn Museum, 1978), 12.

4. Stuart Davis, unpublished letter to Williams, 18 Sept. 1920, Buffalo, F140.

5. Williams, unpublished letter to Kenneth Burke, 27 April 1921, Yale Za 221.

6. Quoted in *Marcel Duchamp*, ed. Anne D'Harnoncourt and Kynaston McShine (New York and Philadelphia: MOMA./Philadelphia Museum of Art, 1973), 279.

7. Ezra Pound, unpublished letter to Williams, 28 Dec. 1922, Buffalo, F520.

8. Robert McAlmon, "Concerning Kora in Hell," *Poetry,* 18 (1921):57–8.

9. D'Harnoncourt and McShine, 251.

10. *The Blind Man,* No. 2 (1917):5.

11. Milton Brown, *American Painting from the Armory Show to the Depression* (Princeton: Princeton U. Press, 1955), 110.

12. Levin, "Wassily Kandinsky and the American avant-garde, 1912–1950," 45.

13. John Cournos, *Autobiography* (New York: G. P. Putnam, 1935), 262.

14. Kandinsky, trans. Sadler, 111–12. Williams need not have read Kandinsky's book to come across these distinctions. As Levin points out, F. J. Mather Jr. cited the relevant passage in a review, "The New Painting and the Musical Fallacy," in *The Nation,* 12 Nov. 1914, 589.

15. Eddy, 124.

16. Marsden Hartley, unpublished letter to Williams, 27 Aug. 1920, Buffalo, F216.

17. Read, *A Concise History of Modern Painting,* 252.

18. Kandinsky, trans. Sadler, 103.

19. Eddy, 136.

20. John Dixon Hunt, " 'Sight and Song Itself': Painting and the Poetry of William Carlos Williams," *Strivers Row,* 1 (1974):104.

21. Quoted in Donald Gallup, "The Weaving of a Pattern: Marsden Hartley and Gertrude Stein," *Magazine of Art,* 41 (1948):257.

22. Hartley, *Adventures in the Arts,* 80.

23. "America, Whitman, and the Art of Poetry," 36.

24. Pound, *Letters,* 123.

25. Hartley to Williams, Buffalo, F216.

26. T. S. Eliot, "Reflections on Contemporary Poetry," *The Egoist,* 4 (1917):151. Williams is not mentioned in the review.

27. Eddy, 118.

28. Ezra Pound, "Irony, Laforgue, and Some Satire," *Poetry,* 11 (1917):96; *Literary Essays,* 283.

29. "America, Whitman, and the Art of Poetry," 28–29.

30. *The Little Review,* 6, No. 1 (May 1919):75.

31. Alfred Kreymborg, *Blood of Things* (New York: N. Brown, 1920), 66–69.

32. Farnham, *Behind a Laughing Mask,* 3; Farnham, Diss., 990.

Chapter 5

1. Haskell, *Marsden Hartley,* 58.

2. Robert McAlmon, unpublished letter to William Carlos Williams, n.d., Buffalo, F 380.

3. McAlmon, "Concerning 'Kora in Hell'," 54–59.

4. Robert McAlmon, *Post Adolescence* (Dijon: Contact Editions, 1923), 17.

5. Robert McAlmon, unpublished letter to William Carlos Williams, 1921, Buffalo, F 362.

6. E. H. Gombrich, *Art and Illusion,* 2nd ed. (1961; rpt. Princeton: Princeton Univ. Press, 1969), 21.

7. Williams, "Gloria," *Others,* 5, No. 6 (1919):3.

8. Harriet Monroe, "A Rhapsodist," *Poetry,* 13 (1918):46.

9. Marsden Hartley, "The Poet of Maine," *The Little Review,* 6, No. 3 (1919):51.

10. Williams, "A Maker," *The Little Review,* 6, No. 4 (1919):37–39. Emily Wallace's note on this essay, that Gould's poetry was "then unpublished except in *Others* and *The Little Review,*" is incorrect; Emily M. Wallace, *A Bibliography of William Carlos Williams* (Middletown, Conn.: Wesleyan University Press, 1968), 173.

11. Paul Rosenfeld, *By Way of Art* (New York: Coward-McCann, 1928), 302.

12. Williams, "From Queens to Cats," *The Dial,* 86 (1929):66–67.

13. Gombrich, 345.

14. Harriet Monroe, "Comment: The Glittering Metropolis," *Poetry,* 14 (1919):30–34.

15. Marsden Hartley, "Dissertation on Modern Painting," *The Nation,* 9 Feb. 1921, 235–36.

16. Paul Rosenfeld, *Port of New York* (New York: Harcourt, Brace, 1924), 92.

17. Hartley, "The Poet of Maine," 53.

18. William Eric Williams, "The House," 3.

19. Hartley, "Dissertation on Modern Painting," 235–36; Williams, "Belly Music," *Others,* 5, No. 6 (1919):26.

20. Haskell, 59.

21. Marsden Hartley, "The Crucifixion of Noël," *The Dial,* 70 (1921):378–80.

22. Williams, "Reader Critic," *The Little Review,* 5, No. 9 (1919):64; not in Wallace, *A Bibliography.*

23. Hartley, "Dissertation on Modern Painting," 236.

24. Williams, "St. Francis Einstein of the Daffodils," *Contact,* No. 4 (1921):2–4.

25. "Société Anonyme, Inc. Report 1920–21," rpt. in *Selected Publications, Société Anonyme* (New York: Arno Press, 1972), 1:11.

26. Williams, "Belly Music," 29.

27. Robert McAlmon, *Being Geniuses Together: 1920–1930,* revised ed. with supplementary chapters by Kay Boyle (Garden City, N.Y.: Doubleday, 1968), 186.

28. Dickran Tashjian, *William Carlos Williams and the American Scene, 1920–1940* (Berkeley: Univ. of Calif. Press; New York: Whitney Museum of American Art, 1978), 71–72; James Guimond, *The Art of William Carlos Williams: A Discovery and Possession of America* (Urbana: Univ. of Illinois Press, 1968), 44; James E. Breslin, "William Carlos Williams and Charles Demuth: Cross Fertilization in the Arts," *JML*, 6 (1977):248–63.

29. Farnham, Diss., 990.

30. Williams, unpublished letter to Henry Wells, 27 July 1955, General Manuscript Collection, Rare Book and Manuscript Library, Columbia University.

31. Robert F. Fleissner points out that in traditional numerological thought five "was the nuptual number, being the union of the first female digit (2) and the first male digit (3)"; "Homage to the Pentad: Williams' "The Great Figure,'" (*NConL*), 1 (1971):3.

32. Leaflet for his April 1916 exhibition at 291, reprinted in *Camera Work,* No. 48 (1916):12.

33. Hartley, April 1916 leaflet.

34. The revisions are discussed by Rod Townley in his *The Early Poetry of William Carlos Williams* (Ithaca, N.Y.: Cornell Univ. Press, 1975), 124–25. Many of Hartley's Berlin paintings are reproduced in Haskell, *Marsden Hartley.*

35. Townley, 125; Breslin, 260.

Chapter 6

1. Pound, *Letters,* p. 73.

2. Pound, *Letters,* p. 166.

3. Else von Freytag-Loringhoven, "Thee I call, 'Hamlet of Wedding-Ring,'" *The Little Review,* 7, No. 4 (1921):48–55; 8, No. 1 (1921):108–11. Williams writes of his disastrous personal involvement with Else, 'The Baroness,' in his autobiography (*Auto,* 164–69).

4. Hartley, *Adventures in the Arts,* 248, 253.

5. Hartley, *Adventures in the Arts,* 242–43, 252, 251.

6. Williams, "Rome," *The Iowa Review,* 9, No. 3 (1978):31–32.

7. Kenneth Burke, unpublished letter to Williams, 3 June 1922, Buffalo, F81.

8. For a full account of *Broom* and *Secession* see Dickran Tashjian, *Skyscraper Primitives* (Middletown, Conn.: Wesleyan Univ. Press, 1975), 116–142.

9. Maxwell Josephson, "The Great American Billposter," *Broom,* No. 3 (1922):305; *Contact,* No. 4 is an "Advertising Number."

10. McAlmon and Boyle, *Being Geniuses Together,* 186.

11. Williams, "Rome," 34.

12. Williams, "Rome," 22.

13. Williams, "Glorious Weather," *Contact,* No. 5 (1923), no page.

14. Williams, "Letter to the editor," *Aesthete 1925,* No. 1 (1925):9–10.

15. Harold Loeb, unpublished letter to Williams, 15 Mar. 1923, Loeb Papers, Firestone Library, Princeton University.

16. Farnham, *Behind A Laughing Mask,* 130.

17. Herbert Read, *A Concise History of Modern Painting,* 3rd ed. (New York: Praeger, 1974), 214–15.

18. In Williams's library, Fairleigh Dickinson University.

19. Maurice Raynal, "Juan Gris," *L'Espirit Noveau,* No. 5 (1921):534–55. The foreword is signed "Vauvrecy," but is the work of Gris: Daniel-Henry Kahnweiler, *Juan Gris: His Life and Work,* trans. Douglas Cooper (New York: Valentin, 1947), 138.

20. Juan Gris, "Notes sur ma peinture," *Der Querschnitt,* Nos. 1–2 (1923):77–78; "Des possibilitiés de la peinture," *The Transatlantic Review,* 1 (1924):482–86, 2 (1924):75–79. All quotations in my text are from Kahnweiler, trans. Cooper.

21. Gris, "Possibilities," Kahnweiler, 139–42.

22. H. D.'s letters to Williams at the French Hospital in 1907 sometimes refer to a "Margaret" (Buffalo, F151–157).

23. Farnham, Diss., 990.

24. Gris, "Notes," Kahnweiler, 138.

25. See, Henry M. Sayre, "Distancing 'The Rose' from *Roses,*" *WCWN,* 5, No. 1 (1979):18–19.

26. My research is confirmed by the current owner, although he notes, "It was reproduced much earlier in photographs of Ms. Stein's apartment. It can be seen on the wall with the other paintings." Harold Diamond, letter to the author, 24 Sept. 1979.

27. Quoted in John Malcolm Brinnin, *The Third Rose: Gertrude Stein and Her World* (Boston: Little, Brown, 1959), 274–75.

28. Gris, "Notes," Kahnweiler, 138.

29. Sherwood Anderson, *Sherwood Anderson's Memoirs,* ed. Ray Lewis White (Chapel Hill: Univ. of North Carolina Press, 1969), xviii–xxii.

30. Paul Rosenfeld, "American Painting," *The Dial,* 71 (1921):651; Pound, although regretting Rosenfeld's verbosity, pressed the editor of *The Dial,* Scofield Thayer, to allow Rosenfeld to write a similar article on American literature. (Nicholas Joost, *Scofield Thayer and The Dial* (Carbondale: Southern Illinois University Press, 1964), 141.)

31. Rosenfeld, "American Painting," 663.

32. Ibid., 658.

33. Ibid., 664.

34. John Marin, unpublished letter to Williams, 6 Mar. 1922, Buffalo, F391.

35. John Marin, "Notes (Autobiographical)," *Manuscripts,* No. 2 (1922):5.

36. Paul Rosenfeld, unpublished letter to Alfred Kreymborg, 27 June 1926, Kreymborg Papers, University of Virginia; Williams, unpublished letter to Robert McAlmon, 9 Mar. 1947, Yale Za 221.

37. Rosenfeld, "American Painting," 663.

38. Williams, "America, Whitman, and the Art of Poetry," 29.

39. For discussion of the "descent" myth in Williams see James E. Breslin, *William Carlos Williams: An American Artist* (New York: O.U.P., 1970), 58–60.

40. It would be interesting to know how much of *Spring and All* is a response to *The Waste Land* (Eliot's poem had appeared in *The Dial* of November 1922). In two letters to Pound written in this month (Lilly Library, Indiana) Williams makes no mention of the work. Cf. *IAG*, 214: "From a low position it is impossible to answer those who know all the Latin and some of the Sanskrit names, much French and perhaps one or two other literatures," and *Pat*, 2: "A reply to Greek and Latin with the bare hands."

41. Charles Demuth, unpublished letters to Williams, 13 Oct. 1921, 9 June 1922, Buffalo F144–45; Farnham, Diss., 990.

42. Quoted in Farnham, *Behind a Laughing Mask*, 136.

43. Hartley, *Adventures in the Arts*, 178.

44. *The Dial* often carried notice of boxing events. In its October 1921 issue Chinese poems translated by Amy Lowell were followed by a series of William Gropper drawings that included one of a boxing match.

45. Williams, "When Fresh, It Was Sweet," *The Dial*, 73 (1922):617–19; not in Wallace, *A Bibliography*. The full text is reprinted in my "Two New Williams Citations," *WCWR*, 6, No. 2 (1980):27–30.

46. Williams, unpublished letters to James Laughlin, 9 Dec. 1937, 26 Mar. 1939, Yale Za 221.

47. Williams, unpublished letter to Louis Untermeyer, July 19, 1924, Untermeyer MSS, Lilly Library, Indiana University, Bloomington.

48. Williams, "Robert McAlmon's Prose," *The Transatlantic Review*, 1 (1924):361–62.

49. Williams, unpublished letter to Monroe Wheeler, Feb. 12, 1923, American Literature MSS, Lilly Library, Indiana.

50. Williams, "America, Whitman, and the Art of Poetry," 29.

51. Robert McAlmon, "What is Left Undone," *The Little Review*, 9, No. 3 (1923):42–43.

Bibliography

Anderson, Sherwood. "The New Note." *The Little Review,* 1, No. 1 (1914):23.

—————. *Sherwood Anderson's Memoirs.* Ed. Ray Lewis White. Chapel Hill: Univ. of North Carolina Press, 1969.

Breslin, James. *William Carlos Williams: An American Artist.* New York: Oxford Univ. Press, 1970.

—————. "William Carlos Williams and Charles Demuth: Cross-Fertilization in the Arts," *JML,* 6 (1977):248–63.

Brinnin, John Malcolm. *The Third Rose: Gertrude Stein and Her World.* Boston: Little, Brown, 1959.

Broom. Ed. Harold Loeb. Rome, Berlin, New York. Vols. 1–5 (1921–24).

Brown, Milton. *American Painting From the Armory Show to the Depression.* Princeton: Princeton Univ. Press, 1955.

Burke, Kenneth. Letter to William Carlos Williams. 3 June 1922. Poetry Collection. SUNY Buffalo.

Contact. Ed. Robert McAlmon and William Carlos Williams. New York. Nos. 1–5 (1920–23).

Cournos, John. *Autobiography.* New York: G. P. Putnam, 1935.

Davis, Stuart. Letter to William Carlos Williams. 18 Sept. 1920. Poetry Collection, SUNY Buffalo.

Demuth, Charles. Letters to William Carlos Williams. 13 Oct. 1921. 9 June 1922. Poetry Collection, SUNY Buffalo.

De Zayas, Marius. "The New Art in Paris." *The Forum,* 45 (1911):180–88.

D'Harnoncourt, Anne, and Kynaston McShine. *Marcel Duchamp.* New York and Philadelphia: Moma/Philadelphia Museum of Art, 1973.

Diamond, Harold. Letter to the author. 24 Sept. 1979.

Dijkstra, Bram. *The Hieroglyphics of a New Speech: Cubism, Stieglitz, and the Early Poetry of William Carlos Williams.* Princeton: Princeton Univ. Press, 1969.

—————. ed. *A Recognizable Image: William Carlos Williams on Art and Artists.* New York: New Directions, 1978.

Doolittle, Hilda. *End to Torment.* Ed. by Norman Holmes Pearson and Michael King. New York: New Directions, 1979.

Eddy, A. J. *Cubists and Post-Impressionism.* Chicago: A. C. McClurg, 1914.

Eliot, T. S. "Reflections on Contemporary Poetry." *The Egoist,* 4 (1917):151.

Farnham, Emily. "Charles Demuth, His Life, Psychology, and Works." Diss. Ohio State, 1959.

—————. *Charles Demuth: Behind a Laughing Mask.* Norman: Univ. of Oklahoma Press, 1971.

Flint, F. S. "The History of Imagism." *The Egoist,* 2 (1915):70–71.

Gallup, Donald. "The Weaving of a Pattern: Marsden Hartley and Gertrude Stein." *Magazine of Art*, 41 (1948):256–61.

Gombrich, E. H. *Art and Illusion*. Rev. ed., 1961; rpt. Princeton: Princeton Univ. Press, 1969.

Guimond, James. *The Art of William Carlos Williams: A Discovery and Possession of America*. Urbana: Univ. of Illinois Press, 1968.

Hartley, Marsden. Letter to Alfred Stieglitz. 1 Feb. 1917. Stieglitz Archive. Beinecke Library, Yale.

————. "The Poet of Maine." *The Little Review*, 6, No. 3 (1919):51–55.

————. Letter to William Carlos Williams. 27 Aug. 1920. Poetry Collection. SUNY Buffalo.

————. "Dissertation on Modern Painting." *The Nation*, 9 Feb. 1921, 235–36.

————. *Adventures in the Arts*. New York: Boni and Liveright, 1921.

Hartpence, Alanson. Letter to William Carlos Williams. n.d. Poetry Collection. SUNY Buffalo.

Haskell, Barbara. *Marsden Hartley*. New York: Whitney Museum of American Art/New York Univ. Press, 1980.

Hulme, T. E. *Speculations*. Ed. by Herbert Read. New York: Harcourt, Brace, 1924.

————. *Further Speculations*. Ed. by Sam Hynes. Minneapolis: Univ. of Minnesota Press, 1955.

Hunt, John Dixon. " 'Sight and Song Itself': Painting and the Poetry of William Carlos Williams. *Strivers Row*. 1 (1974): 77–106

Joost, Nicholas. *Scofield Thayer and the Dial*. Carbondale: Southern Illinois Univ. Press, 1964.

Kahnweiler, Daniel-Henry. *Juan Gris: His Life and Work*. Trans. by Douglas Cooper. New York: Valentin, 1947.

Kandinsky, Wassily. *The Art of Spiritual Harmony*. Trans. by M. T. Sadler. London: Constable, 1914.

————. "Inner Necessity." Trans. by Edward Wadsworth. *Blast*, No. 1 (1914): 119–25.

Kreymborg, Alfred. *Blood of Things*. New York: N. Brown, 1920.

————. *Troubadour*. New York: Boni and Liveright, 1925.

Kunitz, J. and Howard Haycroft, eds. "Mikhail Artsybashev." *Twentieth Century Authors*. New York: H. W. Wilson, 1951.

Lane, John. *Stuart Davis: Art and Art Theory*. Brooklyn, N.Y.: Brooklyn Museum, 1978.

Levin, Sandra Gail. "Wassily Kandinsky and the American Avant-Garde, 1912–1950." Ph.D. diss., Rutgers, 1976.

Lewis, Wyndham. "Editorial." *Blast*, No. 2 (1915):5–6.

————. "A Review of Contemporary Art." *Blast*, No. 2 (1915):38–47.

The Little Review. Ed. by Margaret Anderson and Jane Heap. Chicago, New York. Vols. 1–12 (1914–29).

Loeb, Harold. Letter to William Carlos Williams. 15 Mar. 1923. Loeb Papers. Firestone Library, Princeton.

MacGowan, C. J. "Two New Williams Citations," *WCWR*, 6, No. 2 (1980):27–30.

Marin, John. Letter to William Carlos Williams. 6 Mar. 1922. Poetry Collection. SUNY Buffalo.

———— "Notes (Autobiographical)," *Manuscripts*, No. 2 (1922):5.

Mather, F. J., Jr. "The New Painting and the Musical Fallacy." *The Nation*, 12 Nov. 1914, 588–90.

McAlmon, Robert. "Concerning Kora in Hell." *Poetry*, 18 (1921):54–59.

————. Letters to William Carlos Williams. n.d., 1921. Poetry Collection. SUNY Buffalo.

—————. "What is Left Undone." *The Little Review,* 9, No. 3 (1923):32–43.

—————. *Post-Adolescence.* Dijon: Contact Editions, 1923.

—————, and Kay Boyle. *Being Geniuses Together: 1920–1930.* Rev. ed. Garden City, N.Y.: Doubleday, 1968.

Monroe, Harriet. "Comment: The Glittering Metropolis." *Poetry,* 14 (1919):30–36.

Movius, Geoffrey H. "Caviar and Bread: Ezra Pound and William Carlos Williams, 1902–1914." *JML,* 5 (1976):383–406.

Others. Ed. by Alfred Kreymborg, William Carlos Williams, *et al.* New York, Chicago. Vols. 1–5 (1915–19).

Pound, Ezra. *The Spirit of Romance.* 1910; rpt. New York: New Directions, 1980.

—————. Letters to Isabel Pound. 12 Mar. 1910. 1911. 26 Mar. 1911. 16 May 1911. 20 Jan. 1914. Pound Collection. Beinecke Library, Yale.

—————. Letters to Homer Pound. May 1911. Oct. 1915. Pound Collection. Beinecke Library, Yale.

—————. Letters to William Carlos Williams. 26 Oct. 1912. 28 Dec. 1922. Poetry Collection, SUNY Buffalo.

—————. "How I Began." *T.P.'s Weekly,* 6 June 1913, 707.

—————. "The Tempers." *The New Freewoman,* 1 (1913):227.

—————. "Edward Wadsworth, Vorticist." *The Egoist,* 1 (1914):306–7.

—————. "Arnold Dolmetsch." *The Egoist,* 4 (1917):104–5.

—————. Letter to Alfred Kreymborg. 1922. Kreymborg Papers. Univ. of Virginia.

—————. *Personae: The Collected Poems of Ezra Pound.* 1926; rpt. New York: New Directions, 1950.

—————. Letter to Alfred Stieglitz. 20 Dec. 1934. Stieglitz Archive. Beinecke Library, Yale.

—————. "Teacher's Mission," *English Journal (College Edition),* 23 (1934):630.

—————. *The Letters of Ezra Pound: 1907–1941.* Ed. by D. D. Paige. New York: Harcourt, Brace, 1950.

—————. *Literary Essays of Ezra Pound.* Ed. by T. S. Eliot. London: Faber, 1954.

—————. *Gaudier-Brzeska.* 1916; rpt. New York: New Directions, 1970.

—————. *Selected Prose 1909–1965.* Ed. by W. Cookson. New York: New Directions, 1973.

—————. *Collected Early Poems of Ezra Pound.* Ed. by Michael John King. New York: New Directions, 1976.

—————. *Ezra Pound and the Visual Arts.* Ed. by Harriet Zinnes. New York: New Directions, 1980.

Read, Herbert. *A Concise History of Modern Painting.* New York: Praeger, 1959.

Rosenfeld, Paul. "American Painting." *The Dial,* 71 (1921):649–70.

—————. *Port of New York.* New York: Harcourt, Brace, 1924.

—————. Letters to Alfred Kreymborg. 27 June 1926. 3 Dec. 1931. Kreymborg Papers, Univ. of Virginia.

—————. *By Way of Art.* New York: Coward-McCann, 1928.

Sayre, Henry M. "Distancing 'The Rose' from *Roses,*" *WCWN,* 5, No. 1 (1979):18–19.

—————. *The Visual Text of William Carlos Williams.* Champaign: Univ. of Illinois Press, 1983.

Selz, Peter. *German Expressionist Painting.* Berkeley: Univ. of Calif. Press, 1957.

The Soil. Ed. by Robert Coady. New York. Nos. 1–5 (1916–17).

Stieglitz, Alfred. Letter to Ezra Pound. 3 Nov. 1915. Stieglitz Archive. Beinecke Library, Yale.

Sutton, Denys. *Nocturne: The Art of James McNeill Whistler.* London: Country Life, 1963.

Tashjian, Dickran. *William Carlos Williams and the American Scene, 1920–1940*. Berkeley and New York: Univ. of Calif. Press and Whitney Museum of American Art, 1978.

————. *Skyscraper Primitives*. Middletown, Conn.: Wesleyan Univ. Press, 1975.

Townley, Rod. *The Early Poetry of William Carlos Williams*. Ithaca, N.Y.: Cornell Univ. Press, 1975.

Wallace, Emily M. *A Bibliography of William Carlos Williams*. Middletown, Conn.: Wesleyan Univ. Press, 1968.

Williams, William Carlos. Letter to Mrs. W. G. Williams. 18 April 1904. Williams Collection. Beinecke Library, Yale.

————. Letters to Edgar Williams. 13 Oct. 1904. 21 Aug. 1908. 21 Oct. 1908. 6 April 1909. Williams Collection. Beinecke Library, Yale.

————. "A Selection from 'The Tempers.' *The Poetry Review*, 1 (1912):481–84.

————. Letters to Viola Jordan. 7 June 1914. 11 June 1914. Viola Jordan Papers. Beinecke Library, Yale.

————. "The Great Sex Spiral, A Criticism of Miss Marsden's 'Lingual Psychology' Chapter 1." *The Egoist*, 4 (1917):46.

————. "The Great Sex Spiral, A Criticism of Miss Marsden's 'Lingual Psychology.' " *The Egoist*, 4 (1917):110–111.

————. "America, Whitman, and the Art of Poetry." *The Poetry Review*, 8, No. 1 (1917):27–36.

————. Letter to Edmund Brown. 27 Jan. 1919. Univ. of Virginia.

————. Letter to Kenneth Burke. 27 April 1921. Williams Collection. Beinecke Library, Yale.

————. Letter to Monroe Wheeler. Feb. 1923. American Lit. MSS, Lilly Library, Indiana Univ.

————. Letter to Louis Untermeyer. 1924. Untermeyer MSS, Lilly Library, Indiana Univ.

————. "Robert McAlmon's Prose." *The Transatlantic Review*, 1 (1924):361–64.

————. "Letter to the editor." *Aesthete 1925*, No. 1 (1925):9–10.

————. *In the American Grain*. 1925; rpt. New York: New Directions, 1966.

————. Letters to James Laughlin. 9 Dec. 1937. 26 Mar. 1939. Williams Collection. Beinecke Library, Yale.

————. Letter to Robert McAlmon. 9 Mar. 1947. Williams Collection. Beinecke Library, Yale.

————. *The Collected Earlier Poems of William Carlos Williams*. New York: New Directions, 1951.

————. *The Autobiography of William Carlos Williams*. New York: Random House, 1951.

————. *Selected Essays of William Carlos Williams*. New York: Random House, 1954.

————. Letter to Henry Wells. 27 July 1955. General MSS, Rare Book Library, Columbia University.

————. *The Selected Letters of William Carlos Williams*. Ed. by John C. Thirlwall. New York: McDowell, Obolensky, 1957.

————. "The Lost Poems of William Carlos Williams or The Past Recaptured." *New Directions 16* (1957):3–45.

————. Letter to Norman Holmes Pearson. 20 Sept. 1957. Williams Collection. Beinecke Library, Yale.

————. *I Wanted to Write a Poem: The Autobiography of the Works of a Poet*. Reported and edited by Edith Heal. 1958; rev. ed. New York: New Directions, 1967.

————. "Min Schleppner." *MR*, 3 (1962):324.

————— . *Pictures from Brueghel.* New York: New Directions, 1962.

————— . *Paterson.* New York: New Directions, 1963.

————— . *The Collected Later Poems of William Carlos Williams.* New York: New Directions, 1963.

————— . *Imaginations.* Ed. by Webster Schott. New York: New Directions, 1970.

————— . *The Embodiment of Knowledge.* Ed. by Ron Loewinsohn. New York: New Directions, 1974.

————— . "Rome." Ed. by Steven Ross Loevy. *The Iowa Review,* 9, No. 3 (1978):1–65.

Williams, William Eric. "The House." *WCWN,* 5, No. 1 (1979):1–5.

Wright, Willard Huntington. "What is Modern Painting?" *The Forum Exhibition of Modern American Painters.* New York: Mitchell Kennerley, 1916, 13–24.

Yeats, W. B. *Responsibilities and Other Poems.* London: Macmillan, 1916.

Index